THE "GIFT" OF HEALING

How to Receive and Use Your Natural Healing Powers

By Gerald M. Loe

TOP OF THE MOUNTAIN PUBLISHING
Largo, Florida 34643-5117 U.S.A.

COVER DESIGN
The cover design, depicting the "Gift" of healing, shows the descending dove of Love, Light, or the Spirit, and the Spark of Life, the Energy. The cover design is by Dr. Tag Powell. The *Art* is a "gift" from nature, for it is light reflecting through a drop of water.
HE/SHE
A generic "He" has been used throughout this book, in place of he/she, in order to facilitate your reading speed and increase your concentration efforts. Your understanding is appreciated.

Text Copyright © 1990 by Gerald M. Loe

All rights reserved. No part of this book may be reproduced or utilized in any form or by any means, electronic or mechanical, including photocopying, recording, or by any information storage and retrieval system, without the permission *in writing* from the publisher.

Published by *Top Of The Mountain Publishing*
11701 South Belcher Road, Suite 123
Largo, Florida 34643-5117 U.S.A.

Library of Congress Cataloging-in-Publication Data
Loe, Gerald M. -
    The "Gift" of Healing

    1. Healing.   2. Self-Care, Health
    I. Title
BZ403.L04 1990   651.8'51   90-12355

Manufactured in the United States of America

FOREWORD

How often, when a loved one was ill, have you said, "I just wish there was something I could do to help." Many people would like to help themselves and others, if only they knew how.

You hold in your hands the answer: a step-by-step guide to learning how to receive and use the natural gift of healing.

Our mental and physical abilities to heal the body are accepted today by most members of the medical community. Books like *Love, Medicine and Miracles* by Bernie Segal, and *An Anatomy of an Illness* by Norman Cousins, have fast become million sellers. Dr. O. Carl Simonton's groundbreaking work, using visualization to reduce cancer, *Getting Well Again*, has received well-deserved national attention. This healer's handbook, *The "Gift" of Healing*, will give you the understanding of how these *miracles* occur, and takes you a step further by describing actual proven techniques you can use to help yourself and others.

The author, Gerald Loe, is a practicing healer, and a master healing trainer, who has healed and trained thousands on radio, TV, and in his free healing clinic, which has been in operation for ten years.

I heard of Gerald Loe about 30 years ago, and have been corresponding with him for the past ten years. He is truly an amazing man: an engineer for Zenith Corporation for twenty-five years, an inventor, writer, puzzle originator and, of course, a master healer. You will thoroughly enjoy his story at the back of this book.

Gerald Loe firmly believes that anyone who truly cares for another human being can receive and use these natural healing abilities. We all have them; but most of us go through life without learning how to use them. When I first heard that Gerald was writing this book, I was delighted. At last, a book for everyone who would like to heal themselves and others, to relieve some of the sickness and suffering on this planet.

Do these techniques work? Well, besides the fact that they have been tested for over ten years, I used healing visualization to cure myself of a bone disease which had me crippled for over fifteen years. After seven operations and several types of radiation treatments, I was told that my leg must be amputated. As a last resort, I used the healing visualization similar to what you will learn in this book. Today, and for the past fifteen years, I have had a complete recovery and I lead a normal life using both legs.

I know it works. Now it's your turn to use and enjoy your gift, and make a difference in your world. All you have to do is care, and follow these instructions.

Enjoy,

Dr. Tag Powell

DEDICATION

This book is dedicated to my several spirit guides, who have taught me so much in my attempts to teach others; with special thanks to my brother Ronald, who has been guiding me for several years; and to Padre Pio, who baptized me with the Holy Spirit and has been guiding me ever since, and has thus increased all my abilities.

I would also like to thank my wife Phyllis, and my friend Helen Kelly, for their help in bringing this work to the public.

THIS BOOK IS CHARGED WITH ENERGY!

To help you more readily realize the presence of this wonderful force, THIS BOOK IS CHARGED WITH ENERGY! Perhaps you have already felt it as you hold this book; possibly the energy charge drew your attention to the book in the first place. If you are one of the doubters who believes that there is no energy charge because you cannot feel it, just check it out by handing it to a young child and ask him or her what it feels like. In most cases it will be felt as a tingling.

How can this be accomplished? Obviously I did not stand at the end of an assembly line and handle every book. That is not necessary. This book will show you how energy follows the thoughts and decisions we make, and this charge is part of the proof of those ideas.

Basically, all I did was to decide that each copy of this book would be charged with energy to help the reader become a better healer or to become a better person in any way that he/she desires. In my mind, I see this goal achieved, and thank God that it is so. There is enough energy in God's universe to keep it charged without loss, and so shall it be!

May you all be blessed by it!

Gerald M. Loe

TABLE OF CONTENTS

Chapter One
The Healing Force

Chapter Two
Seven Methods of Channeling Energy

Chapter Three
Seventeen Special Healing Techniques

Chapter Four
Mental Detection and Correction of Problems

Chapter Five
Other Pathways to Healing

Chapter Six
Further Tips on Healing, and Miscellany

Chapter Seven
Healing Past Lives

CHAPTER ONE
The Healing Force

CHAPTER ONE
The Healing Force

In *First Corinthians, 12th Chapter,* Paul lists the "Gifts of the Spirit." While it is common for these abilities to be considered as gifts, there are some of us who feel they are not free gifts, but have to be earned in some way or another. In other words, if you are born with a certain gift, this really means that you earned or developed that gift in your past, and have simply come back with it in order to continue using it. This, of course, refers to reincarnation and past lives. While this is not intended to be a treatise on reincarnation and past lives, it is a fact that memories of past lives can be elicited in most people by the use of sometimes simple and sometimes complex techniques. At times, it is as natural to a person as yesterday's memories. Frequently, young children will tell you about "when I was here before," if carefully questioned, and not condemned for "telling those lies."

At any rate, the ability or "gift" has to start somewhere, and I believe the work to develop it can be shortened somewhat and the path made smoother by the proper commitments to be a channel for God's blessings, and applying yourself where you are *now*. The famous psychic, Edgar Cayce, often told people, "work where you are."

This means to use the abilities you have right now; dedicate them to God, and use them to help yourself and others around you. If you do this, you will increase your abilities at intervals as you work, and grow into greater service. A little work done by following the material in this book will probably show you that you *do* have abilities that you never dreamed you had, once they are brought to your attention.

One of the gifts of the Spirit listed by St. Paul is that of healing. My own abilities in this direction have increased tremendously in the last few years and, as a result, I have been teaching many people how to become channels for healing. I was not born with this ability, but developed it with loving application. I believe we are all born with the *potential* to develop in this direction.

There are actually many people involved in Spiritual or Psychic healing, using many different approaches, and a large number of books have been written on the subject. I believe, however, that although each has served its' special purpose to a degree, most of them have fallen short in some way. By not being able to *demonstrate* the healing power, many books don't show the reader exactly what to do to be an effective channel. Many authors are limited in their views. Many healers, similarly, are bound by their own beliefs and cannot understand or accept another's methods.

It has been brought to my attention that there are a great many differing concepts of what constitutes Spiritual Healing. Proponents of one discipline frequently look down on all other methods as being false or wrong, and not the "real" or "proper" healing system, as is their method.

Many people have told me that some psychic has mentioned to them that they should be doing healing, but that they had no idea of how to go about becoming a healer. Some of you undoubtedly fall in that category, so this is your chance to achieve some proficiency in the art. Even if you are not intending to become a healer, the knowledge in this book can enable you to achieve many things more easily, since healing is really CREATION.

Each one of us, *right now*, has many more abilities than we ever dreamed of, and we are just waiting for someone to say, "Did you know that you can do........(a latent ability) right now, without special training? Here is how you can do it..." And so we can!

I attended a workshop on healing sponsored by Spiritual Frontiers Fellowship, conducted by a nationally known Methodist pastor who has been in the healing ministry for some time. I was volunteering some information and demonstrating the energy flows of an individual before the group, whereupon the conductor said, "But we are dealing here with two entirely different things. What you are doing is merely 'magnetic' healing. What we are doing is entirely different, and there is nothing *flowing* when we do it. What we are doing is *spiritual* healing."

Therefore, I realized the need for an integrated study of some of the methods, to show the unity behind them all. Such an understanding should lead to better cooperation between healing channels of various disciplines, and perhaps increase the percentage of successful healings.

Magnetic Healing

It is unfortunate that the label *magnetic* has been put on some of the methods of handling life energy. The term implies that the acting force is akin to the physical description of magnetism, with its' physical limitations. A few selective experiments with a sensitive psychic motor, such as my ENERGY WHEEL®, can prove that this moving force, which is capable of moving matter and which can be directed by the mind, can *not* be identified correctly as the action of heat (either by radiation or convection currents), electricity, magnetism, or gravitation. Therefore, since it can not be classified by classical science, it has been largely ignored by classical scientists.

Such an opinion is hardly scientific. There have been a few from time to time who have ventured into research of this life energy, but their efforts have either been laughed at by their peers, or else kept secret for fear of ridicule. Look at what happened to William Reich; he was persecuted by the government for his claims about orgone, which is the same energy that we are talking about.

You and I can prove that magnetic healing works over a distance as well as up close to the body; therefore it is not magnetic at all. Let us then drop the term "magnetic healing" and just refer to it as "healing." I shall attempt to show that all methods are basically the same, if they are methods that work. All healing is Spiritual Healing, in the deepest analysis. There is only ONE healing force in the Universe, and that is this Creative Force that we will be discussing in this book.

Some "authorities" have said that there are different kinds of healing forces, differentiating between magnetic healing, magnetic passes, the Christ Force, Jesus, Buddha, Allah, etc. It is my claim that they are all the same force, seen through different eyes and minds. Each person with a particular belief or expectation finds that his method works, so he assumes that his concept is *the* correct one.

The Creative Force

There is ample evidence, however, that this Creative Force follows thoughts put into it, dependent upon faith or belief, which is part of the thought pattern of the user. This means that the energy follows the expectations *and* limitations of the thought pattern of each user, and thereby creates the illusion of a number of healing forces, each with its' own characteristics.

Thus our healing energy can act as if it spins, when required. It can vibrate, if necessary. It can be stored in objects, people, or just in space itself. It can be handled as if it were "positive" or "negative," and thus flowed as if it had polarity. Some healers say that the right hand has one type of energy, differing from that of the left hand, and for them it is so. We can produce either type from either hand, however, or without the hands, just by putting the proper thoughts behind the energy as we use it. You don't have to believe me; just try it for yourself.

What happens in the ordinary healing of a wound? The subconscious mind of the patient controls the automatic functioning of the body, and directs the regenerative processes to repair and grow the cells back together, to throw off poisons and waste materials, bringing food to the cells through the blood supply, to reunite the injured area according to a pattern which exists somewhere within the person. The physical body structure follows this invisible pattern body. If the pattern body is in good order the wound will heal perfectly. If the pattern is defective, possibly changed by traumatic events or other mental attitudes, the healing will not be perfect. In fact, it is possible there will be no healing, no matter what medications are given, if the pattern has been sufficiently altered. Experiments with autosuggestion have shown that scarring can be minimized or eliminated by the proper mental attitudes; by building up the proper mental pictures in the patient's mind.

Now what happens when a healer lays a hand on the wound or says a prayer to help it? He flows extra energy to the patient, and holds a mental picture of health as he does it, seeing the patient healthy. He is projecting this pattern of thought to the pattern body of the patient, thinking, "Make it like this!" This is done with the *expectation* of that pattern being accepted. The time it takes for the healing to occur will depend upon a number of factors, such as a willingness to change the thought pattern that brought the problem originally, feelings of guilt and the need for suffering, and the whole belief structure of the hurt individual.

Space and Time

Now consider this carefully: The subconscious mind is not limited by space or time. Both are transcended in dreams, for example. Space and time are both conscious mind concepts or agreements. The healing processes are handled by the subconscious mind; therefore, in some instances, healing can be *instantaneous*, from the conscious mind's viewpoint!

In assisting the healing process, we can gather and flow this life energy, which is creative, to the patient. As I do this process, I visualize the wound being healed. This is merely one of the many ways it can be handled. Instead of flowing the energy *through* me, I can visualize the energy being gathered to the wound, flowing in from around the patient, with the same visualization of health.

Consider that your soul (and everyone else's soul) is already occupying all space and all time! In a sense, this is precisely the same as laying your physical hand on the patient. The distance does not make any difference. Since this book tells you how to do this yourself, you can do the same things, if you try it and work at it. The point I wish to emphasize is that we do not have to have the healing energy flow through our own bodies to send to another, but just visualizing it being there in the patient will *cause* it to be there.

Now let us look at an instance of healing where

the healing channel merely holds the thought of the patient in loving prayer, and the patient is thereby healed. I contend that, to be effective, this prayer must contain a picture or concept of perfection of the patient, and it is this perfect picture, coupled with the desire and expectation of healing, which flows God's creative forces through the patient (who must be receptive to it) and manifests the healing. As you can see, from this viewpoint, essentially the same method is being used as in the other earlier examples.

The following occurrence tends to confirm the above view. I spoke with a charismatic healer who was the student of the nationally known Methodist minister mentioned previously. She told me that on occasion, when a child is sick or injured, she will take the child in her arms to heal it. Sometimes she will forget to open herself to the inflow of God's healing power, and thus drain her own energy to the child. Following such a happening, she has to regain her own strength. When she *thinks* about opening herself to the influx of God's energy, she is not depleted; the power just flows through her to the patient. So again, the same basic method is being used, and only the outer handling is different.

Let us consider another healing technique. In the history of hypnotism, you can read of Mesmer and the cures he was able to produce with his techniques, some of them due to "magnetic passes" near the patient and others by stroking with magnets. He constructed a device known as a *baquet* which, as I understand it, was a tub containing magnets, with wires leading from them to each of the patients, thus allowing several people to be treated at the same time. This was quite effective, and many cures were claimed.

As will be discussed later, the healing energy is at any place where it is visualized or expected (the same thing, really); therefore, when a magnet is considered a source of healing, it is that. "Ask, and it shall be given!" When the tub of magnets with their wires is considered to be the source of healing, it becomes that source of the healing energy.

A healing shrine becomes such because of the holiness or healing quality attributed to it. By considering it holy, you thereby draw the Holy Spirit or healing energy to it. If people were to come to full realization of this, they could create powerful healing shrines in their own homes. What makes you think that one place on earth is holier than another? Moses was told, "The place where you stand is holy ground," and that means *wherever you* stand, for all is the creation of God.

One book published on psychic healers states that a healing is considered a spiritual healing only if the healer is not depleted by the process. Not so! Depletion is caused by using your own body energy instead of channeling or plugging into God's Universal Supply, which is limitless.

You *can* use your body energy for healing and then recharge your body, but this method could be harder on you, especially if you are inexperienced. When you are drained, you are more likely to become ill yourself. I would not recommend this method (using your own body energy) for most persons. Most persons are not taking the proper responsibility for their own health, but are instead blaming their ills on weather changes or on ill people with whom they are coming into contact.

The permanence of a healing is considered by some to be a criterion of spiritual healing. But how many of us are healed of ALL of our illnesses at the same time? A person may grow out of the need to have a certain illness, then receive a healing. He may then re-create the same illness because of another "fault" in his nature which needs resolution. To some people this would seem like a reversion to the former illness, when in reality it would be a progression, a sign of growth showing that he is now ready for another step in his total healing. In other words, each illness can have a number of causes, which are not necessarily all actively functioning at the same time.

Our bodies are the creations of our minds. As long as our minds are not perfect, we will continue to see reflected in our bodies the imperfections within, which are still to be overcome. No matter how miserable or horrible a crippled and distorted body may be, it is still a *perfect creation* of that soul, signifying problems to be eventually overcome. There are *no* accidents in God's Universe!

I was told of a man who had a marvelous healing of cancer through the ministry of the late Kathryn Kuhlman. Two of the man's close relatives, however, constantly ridiculed the idea of such a healing and denied its' reality, until the man was once more taking on the symptoms of the disease. What a man's mind has created once can be created again, if the pattern of his thinking is not permanently changed. It is up to each person to accept or reject the suggestions of others. If only the "man on the street" could be educated to understand that illness is not caused by anything *outside* the person, but instead by what is *inside! And as the source of illness is within, so is the cure.*

All healing is spiritual, regardless of the method of treatment. Healing cannot be forced on anyone; an individual will be healed only when he is ready for it on the deepest level, and the time of readiness may be entirely different from what the conscious mind says. The soul knows when you are ready for healing, knows exactly what changes in thinking and attitudes will be necessary to bring you into proper alignment with God, and its' purposes will not be defeated.

I read of a group of people being taught the "laying on of hands" in plant growth experiments. The results of which were that a percentage of those taught developed a "brown thumb" instead of a green thumb," which meant they had adverse effects upon the plants instead of enhancing their growth and health. I believe that this result was caused by the failure of the instructor to teach certain principles to the students, and that these "negative healers" could be changed to useful channels in a short time. Perhaps they were actually drawing energy from the plants, although it is more likely that their thought patterns needed changing. The crux of the matter is that all forces, including healing energy, can be used positively or negatively. To get the proper effect, you must put the proper thought behind it.

Perhaps you know nothing about healing energy; maybe you have heard about it, but are skeptical and doubt its' existence. On the other hand, you may have been aware of it since you were young. At any rate, it is likely that something in this book will be of great use to you personally, so apply what is given here and test it out.

Since my own abilities to handle energy have increased so greatly, I find it increasingly easy to demonstrate energy flows to those I meet, so they can feel it or see it flow between the hands. It is also possible to demonstrate that this energy is capable of moving matter. I designed and manufacture a small psychic motor known as the ENERGY WHEEL®, which is so sensitive that anyone can move it using life energy from the body. It can be done repeatedly. Simple experiments with it can prove that the motion cannot be explained by such forces as heat, air currents, electricity, or magnetism.

This same energy has been caused to affect a photographic emulsion. Many experimenters have been working with Kirlian photography in studying the energy field around the human body as well as animals and plants, and noting the changes in the aura caused by a healer's flowing energy. To those who would insist that the Kirlian effect is nothing more than a corona discharge, I would state that it is more than corona effect, since the creative energy is able to modify or change the corona flow and produce the same effect as seeing the aura. I have affected my own finger aura prints by projecting healing energy, and I have also increased my wife's auric field (as shown by a Kirlian print) by just deciding to project energy to her as the exposure was being made. It is not difficult to do, as you will probably discover if you try the methods given here.

I intend to show you how to become aware of the

Healing Force, or Holy Spirit, or whatever you wish to call it. I will then show you a number of different ways to channel the energy to yourself and others, and give you information on how to handle it properly.

First, however, I want to make sure that you tune into the proper energy for healing.

SECTION 1:
Getting The Energy You Want

Consider the proposition that, at all times, most people are radiating their thoughts, both positive and negative, plus their emotions, also both positive and negative, in all directions. Time and space are no barriers to these transmissions. In addition to these energies, there is the pure energy from God present everywhere.

Energy is controlled by your thoughts and decisions, both in collection and transmission to another, by you as the healing channel. From the foregoing, you can understand that to pull in and project just plain energy would not be the wisest action. Choose the energy you desire! The closer you can conceive of this energy as being PURE LOVE, the better it is for all healing purposes. You get the energy you ask for and expect. *Therefore, make sure that when you intend to pull in energy for any purpose, you decide that it will be only God's pure energy, and thus it will be so.* Pulling in random energy could bring you problems, especially if you are in an area where there are many emotional and physical disturbances. Always specify in your mind: PURE ENERGY. Practice taking in energy with this thought until it becomes fully automatic.

SECTION 2:
Becoming Aware of
The Healing Energy

The following technique has been very effective in introducing people to healing energy and instructing them in its' proper usage. I used it successfully over radio programs to acquaint the listeners with collecting and channeling healing energy. The first time I tried this, on a Chicago radio program, the results were very evident to the program director and myself. The program director was amazed at the tremendous amount of energy (the result of the listeners channeling healing energy through us to the telephone callers) that was flowing through his hands and the change in the "atmosphere" in the studio. We had been sitting with our palms up. It felt like a very high voltage charge was present in the room. Here is the technique I taught the listeners on that program.

Hold your hands out in front of you, with the palms downward. Put your attention on the feeling in your palms and fingers, noting exactly how they feel. Now turn your hands with the palms facing up. Note the difference in feeling in the palms and fingers, between the two positions. There is a *difference* in energy impinging on the palms when one turns the palms over. Almost everyone can feel a difference, however, the way in which it is felt will vary from one individual to another.

The difference in feeling in the palms or fingers signifying awareness of this energy may be felt in a number of ways, or it may not be felt at all, at first. The highest sense is just to *know* it is there; but most of us have to transform this knowledge down to the equivalent of one of our physical senses so we can feel it, and thereby know it is there. It may be felt as a warmth, as a cool breeze, as a pressure, as a pull, as a vibration or a pulsation, or as a tingle in the fingertips or palms. Children usually feel the tingle very readily. Sometimes the awareness can not be readily described, but it is still there. Regardless of the *type* of difference you feel in your hands as you turn the palms up, that difference you do feel is the result of the energy you are picking up.

The feeling is not due to suggestion; neither is it due to constriction of the nerves or blood vessels. The response is too quick to be associated with that. Extending your hands with the palms up is a symbol of acceptance or receiving.

This energy has been *discovered* many times, and has been given many names. The Sanskrit name is prana; the Hunas of Hawaii call it mana; the AMORC Rosicrucians call it nous; Reichenbach called it odyle or odic force; William Reich called it orgone, and so forth. It is also life force, creative energy, the Christ Force, or the Holy Spirit. Edgar Cayce referred to it as the Creative Force.

I have come to consider it to be the Basic Creative Force of the Universe! It is a force that is capable of affecting anything on any level. That is why it can affect electrical fields (as in Kirlian photography); magnetic fields (move a compass, as Kulagina does); affect other chemical actions (cause or heal ulcers); affect mental processes (heal mental problems and affect meditational abilities), and much more.

You will notice that I said, "cause or heal ulcers." That is because all illness is caused by the misuse of this same energy, in one way or another. Your condition of health is affected by how you use this creative energy in your daily thoughts and actions. Improperly used, it becomes destructive; or more precisely, we would say that negative or disease conditions are created. This is how we create our own future from day to day!

Those who have extensively studied meditation tell us that the ones who meditate with their palms uppermost seem to get more out of meditation than the ones who do it with the palms downward. A good palmist will tell you that when a person shows you his open hands as he talks with you, he is being open with you, for the information about his character is revealed in the lines in his palms. If you are involved in any type of meditation, I would suggest that you try it with your palms upward for some time, if you are not already doing so. See if you can note any significant difference.

If you have a group of people sit with palms uppermost in their laps without telling them the reason for doing so, within a little while most of them will feel a tingle or unusual warmth or one of the other sensations indicating the energy presence, once their attention is called to it. This shows that they are tuning in on this energy to a certain degree just by the act of sitting in this manner. Most people will be unaware of what this feeling means, unless they have had previous experience with it. Of course, the effect is greatly increased by focusing one's attention (and intention) on it, especially if you visualize pulling pure energy into your hands.

After you sit for a few minutes in this manner of taking in energy, you will usually feel an increase of the flow, as your awareness increases. To use this energy for yourself, just accept it with that thought in mind. If you wish, you can send it to any part of your body by simply intending that it go there. ENERGY FOLLOWS THOUGHT! You can take it in to perk you up. You can take it in to balance your energy flows throughout your body. You can take it in to raise your consciousness, especially by flowing it upwards above your head, into the "crown chakra." This is the area associated with haloes.

Do not concentrate on illness, but concentrate on health instead.

If you are one of those relatively insensitive people who cannot feel any energy, you can get a boost in your awareness by having a friend join you in these experiments. There is a "group effect" when you do it with another, which tends to raise the awareness of all the participants.

CHAPTER TWO
Seven Methods of Channeling Energy

CHAPTER TWO
Seven Methods of Channeling Energy

If you are going to be learning to channel energy, you will first need someone to channel to, someone who is able to easily tell whether you are doing it properly or not. Since most people can feel the energy, when shown how to do so, this should not present much of a challenge. Children almost always feel it as a tingle. At any rate, locate a friend who is able to feel the energy, and ask him or her to work with you. I will, for convenience, call this assistant the "subject." The subject may or may not be in need of healing. You will still be able to create effects that can be physically felt.

METHOD 1.
Pulling in Pure Energy

Hold your left hand out with the palm up, and visualize (or think of) pulling in pure energy. Do not make pulling motions with your hands; what we want are mental concepts, not physical motions. Perhaps you will not feel any energy. Do not assume, however, that just because you cannot feel it, it does not exist, or that you cannot become a healing channel. Act as though you *are* a healer, and chances are that your awareness of the energy will increase after you work with it for a while. Such has certainly been the case with me. It used to be that I could not feel the energy at all, whereas now, not only do I feel the energy flow, I even get feedback which tells me that the other person is feeling the flow in some way, too.

Have the subject hold his hands out with their palms up. Aim your right hand at one of his hands, with the intention of flowing the pure energy to him. You may touch his hand and do it by contact if you wish. Flow the energy with the thought of supplying it to fulfill some of his needs. After a moment when you think that this goal has been accomplished, stop what you are doing and what you have been thinking. Wipe your hands together as though you are washing them, with the thought of the goal having been accomplished, and then think of something else. This serves to cut off the healing at its' highest point, to get the best results. It prevents you from unconsciously draining your own life energy to him and thus depleting yourself. It also prevents you from drawing back, along the channel you have established, any of the negative qualities the other person might have. It is similar to taking a picture. You get the person in the proper position for the results you want, with all the desirable qualities. The flash goes off when the shutter is open, and the picture is finished, except for the end result. As you mentally release the picture of healing, it goes to a higher plane of your mind and the subject's mind, to create the healing he is seeking.

If you were to *omit* the *cut-off* in the healing process, it is possible that your thoughts about the patient could dwell upon some less-than-optimum possibilities, and therefore, manifest a less-than-optimum healing, since the channel would still be open.

There are some people who unconsciously absorb energy from the others around them without differentiating between positive and negative energy. That is why I insist upon a definite cut-off to prevent it from ever happening.

After you have practiced this method for a time, flow some energy in this manner: receive energy with your right hand and aim it or touch it with your left hand. Practice both methods. It can be done in any way you can conceive.

By the way, *laying on of hands* is a very limiting concept. A little experimentation will show you that you do not have to touch the subject with your physical hand to effect the healing. We can all touch and be touched through God, regardless of distance. When you become experienced in healing, you will probably be able to project your touch so that a distant person can actually feel it. I can do this with certain people, so I know that others can do it as well. We are all truly together, *right now*, throughout all time and space, through God.

Now, check with your subject and find out what he feels. In a very short time he will probably feel the energy collecting where it is needed. An asthmatic will feel it in the chest almost immediately, as the energy relaxes the muscles to permit easier breathing. A person with tension or soreness in a particular part of the body will usually feel it go there quickly, and feel the tightness start to relax.

A headache can be literally pushed out in very short order, when you get used to flowing the energy. An easy process is to project the energy to the back of the subject's neck, and see it in your mind as pushing the headache and the cause of it out of his head. It usually happens very quickly, unless the person is using the headache to control someone else, and therefore, is not about to part with it.

METHOD 2.
Thought Flow Energy

After you have worked with Method #1 for a while and know that you are doing well with it, try this next method. Check with your subject on the state of your progress.

Decide to receive energy with both hands at once (with palms up), and tell or will the energy to go to your assistant or subject, with the same intentions in mind as when using Method #1. Experiment by projecting energy to various parts of his body, both external and internal. Direct it with your mind alone so he can feel that it is really happening, that the energy follows your thoughts.

Now, to show you the importance of *asking* for the energy, say or think, "Lord, let me flow more of your healing energy," and immediately you will feel an increase of energy. Then, to show you the value of visualization, imagine a veritable "Niagara Falls" of energy pouring in, and again note the increase coming in and flowing to the subject. *Energy follows thought!*

Of course, as you finish each energy "application" to the subject, cut off the flow in the same manner which you were taught in Method #1; *by washing your hands of it.*

METHOD 3.
White Light

After the above has been achieved, the following is the next step I generally use.

Visualize a pure white light from God coming down through the top of your head and going to the subject, following your thoughts as before. You may either direct the energy with one or both hands, with or without touching; or simply conceive of it going where you wish, or wherever it should go to the subject. Focus your thoughts in the same manner as with the other techniques, and close the healing process as usual. Release it!

METHOD 4.
God Energy

Have your subject seated. Stand behind him, and put both hands over his head, but not necessarily touching his head. Hold your hands with the palms down. Visualize a light from above coming down through your hands, entering his head and flowing through his body. You might program this action by saying aloud to him the following, or something similar:

"Visualize with me, a pure white light coming from above, going through my hands and entering you, filling your whole body with the pure light of God. Let it get rid of all the darkness, so that you become radiant with His love. See it increasing all of your abilities and your talents, getting rid of patterns that are negative and no longer useful...decreasing tensions throughout your whole body, creating new patterns of better health and sharper mind...being better able to guide you in your daily living, uniting more closely your consciousness with your inner, higher self...getting rid of doubts...expanding your aura with the love of God...and balancing all your energy flows for better functioning, knowing that God loves you and is always with you."

As you do this you will usually feel the subject's aura expanding or getting stronger. At times it becomes so strong that it almost pushes your hands up higher. As you finish your dialogue, close off the process in the usual manner by brushing your hands together and letting go.

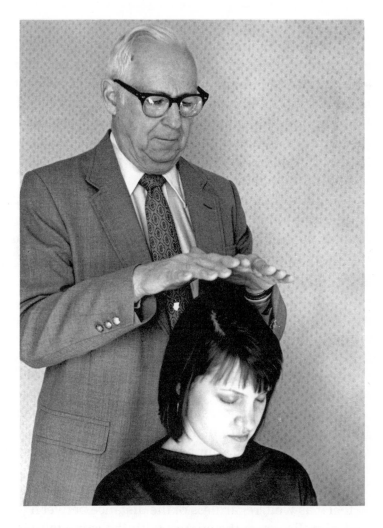

See if you can feel the energy that the
young lady is receiving.

Note that, in this method, you are not flowing the energy through your body. You do not have to feel the energy flowing through your hands, but it is a good way to be sure that the subject is receiving it. If you feel it flowing, you know that he is accepting it. If the subject visualizes or creates a shield between your hands and his head, you will feel the energy flow stop. You can verify this by having him try it.

Once you have used this method of flowing energy to a person, he can re-create the same flow any time he wishes, by merely visualizing the energy coming in again. Verify this by having the subject try it without your hands being there.

METHOD 5.
Energy from a Distance

Here is a slight (but important) variation on the above.

Have the subject seated as before. Stand several feet away from him, or in the next room, and imagine he is in front of you. Put your hands in front of you over his imaginary head, and visualize the white light as before. You will feel it flowing, as previously, and he will be able to feel it as well, regardless of the distance between you and him. Program the energy with the same thoughts that you used before. You will find that you can still feel his aura as though he were actually there. Even though the aura is said to extend only a few inches from the body, it can be felt at any distance, if you wish!

METHOD 6.
Absentee Healing

Have the subject seated as above. Be at a distance, as in Mehtod #5. Without using your hands at all, visualize the same energy entering his head and fulfilling the same purposes as before. Use only your mind. This time you will not have to feel the energy flowing to him. Just *know* he is receiving it. Check to see if he can feel it as he did before. The more energy you can conceive of, the more energy there is. *Energy follows thought!*

Now consider this: Any of these methods can be used in *absent* healing, over any distance. Picture or imagine the person being right in front of you, and flow the energy to him using any of these methods, and you will find that you can do it!

You should bear in mind that as you apply yourself to healing, your abilities will change and expand, so that after a while, the methods that seem challenging now will most likely become easier to do. Explore your talents and limitations at intervals; your learning never stops, unless you stop it. Use the methods that give the best results. Use your intuition as to which method should be used. The important thing to keep in mind is that you should not use your own body energy to send to another. Take extra energy from the Universal Supply which is always all around us, and is always available when we ask for it.

The above ideas are not the ultimate, of course. If the Holy Spirit is everywhere, it is also within your being, *right now*. Our goal should be (whether we are healing channels or not) to become so aware of this internal (and Eternal) presence that we HAVE the energy to give to ourselves or to another instantly, as needed, in any amount. There is an old occult (which merely means "hidden") saying, "All the power that ever was, or will be, is here, NOW!"

METHOD 7.
Proxy Healing

Another method, which might be mentioned here, could be called *proxy healing*. In this method, have the person sitting in the chair think of the person who needs the healing. As an alternative, the proxy can pretend he is the person, instead of being himself. In other words, the proxy identifies with the subject as well as he can. The healer then directs the energy to the proxy as though he were the patient.

The energy will then go to the person he is thinking of or being. When the procedure is completed, the proxy should immediately decide to "be" himself again, to cut off the identification with the other person. Otherwise he may find himself feeling the problems of the person with whom he has been identifying, which can be quite uncomfortable.

Incidentally, you quite often hear the statement, "Nobody can know how I really feel." This statement is *entirely incorrect*. It is being done every day by those who have learned to identify with another.

If the proxy does not know the patient, it still does not make much of a difference. By deciding to do so, he sends energy to the person whose name he has been given. There are no strangers through God.

The amount of physical distance between healer and patient is of no consequence. The strength of the energy does not diminish with distance. Each soul is already in all space and all time. In other words, the energy does not have to travel to a distant place as we ordinarily think of travel. The patient is already with us no matter how distant his physical body is; therefore, when we send healing energy to him, the energy does not have to "go" there, but simply *is* there.

Those who are researching the healing force with the idea that it is an electromagnetic radiation are barking up the wrong tree, since it can easily be proven that this force is not subject to space and time limitations. It does not diminish with distance.

CHAPTER THREE
Seventeen
Special Healing
Techniques

CHAPTER THREE
Seventeen Special Healing Techniques

SECTION 1.
Clearing the Sinuses

The following technique is a rather effective and rapid way to improve blocked sinuses.

Pull in energy with your left hand. Point your right hand at the subject's eye-nose area. Wiggle your fingers together like a fish moving its' tail while swimming; at the same time, mentally direct the energy to move in a like manner throughout the sinus passages, with the purpose of breaking up the blockages and the patterns that caused them. After a couple of seconds of this, bring both of your hands together with the fingertips touching, then draw your hands apart six or eight inches. Before you pull them apart, think of creating a pulling force between the two hands; visualize pulling or drawing energy with each hand, as though your fingertips were connected together with rubber bands.

This method works very well, and an immediate improvement is usually noted; sometimes a handkerchief is needed at once as the sinuses start to drain. Even a person who has no sinus problems can feel the effects of what you are doing. This method works well at a distance, just by picturing the person being before you. The hardest part of this is in describing exactly what it feels like as you draw your hands apart.

Remember, the effect you wish to achieve is that of pulling the sinus passages open; pretend you are doing just that. If you feel the energy flowing when you do it, you know that person is receiving it. Check this method on a friend. If it works, use it.

(The material in this book is going to seem downright impossible to some. That's all right. You do not have to believe everything that is written. You can test these methods for yourself, and *know* that they work. Dare to try them! Break out of your ruts!)

SECTION 2.
A General Purpose Cleansing Spin

Here is how to use an *energy spin* for general improvement. Stand either in front of or behind the subject. Pull in energy with one hand. Point your other hand down toward the subject's feet, and raise your arm slowly, until it has pointed above his head after traversing the length of his body, about three or four seconds for the complete movement. As you do this, create with your mind a large counterclockwise spin; similar to a large doughnut or wheel of energy, which is visualized to follow the movement of your hand up around his body, starting with his feet and ending with his head, or just above it. Then lower your arm, and start at the feet again with another spin; raise it up the body again, and repeat for a few minutes. The purpose of this rising spin (which should be seen in your mind as you do it), should be to break loose the patterns of illness that are present, whether you know what they are or not; and also to revitalize the various chakras or control centers of the body, which are connected with psychic or spiritual development, as well. A good book on Yoga will be able to give you more information on the chakras if you are interested.

At any rate, most people can feel this rising spin and its effects, and can also cause others to feel it. Some feel it as a tingle going up the spine, while others may feel it differently. This can also be done at a distance, by visualizing the person as standing in front of you. It makes no difference whether the person is actually standing, sitting, or lying down at the time you are working on him. Of course, small spins may be used in a particular part of the body, whenever you feel they are appropriate. Instead of spinning, you can also vibrate the energy in various directions. Use your intuition for the proper method to be applied in each case.

SECTION 3.
Drawing Out Irritants

This is a method for reducing irritation in a part of the body. It is done by drawing the fingers near the skin in a sort of combing motion, as though you are combing out snarls or foreign matter. At the end of each stroke or pass, the fingers are flicked past the thumb, or shaken, as though any material combed out is, by this motion, shaken loose from the fingers before making the next pass. Do not omit this cleansing thought and shake.

The above is the physical part of the picture. The most important part of the process is what you are doing mentally as you do the above. That is: Visualize your fingers extending down through the flesh of the subject, and into the congested area, thereby pulling all the irritants out. THINK the pull, as in clearing the sinuses. The subject will usually feel the pull when you are doing it correctly. As you do this, visualize the irritants being removed, leaving the area clean and healthy. When I feel the goal has been accomplished, I usually finish by running my hand parallel to the surface, and visualize my hand soothing and smoothing the area, inside and outside. See the area being healthy and whole. I have used this method successfully for such things as sore muscles, chest congestion, headaches, itching caused by improper intravenous congestion, operation incisions, negative side effects from medication, and more. It works at a distance as well, by just imagining the subject in front of you. Create the pull with your mind, and it will be there.

There is one caution to observe. Do not mentally pull with all your might, or it could make the subject uncomfortable. Instead, think of removing the irritants gently, with love, as though it were easy to do. The reality of this method is illustrated in the following example.

I had taught my healing class the technique. Later, one of the ladies reported that she was using it to remove a headache from her daughter. She was pulling with all her might, until her daughter said, "Ouch, Ma! You're pulling too hard. It feels as though you're pulling my brains out!"

Properly developed, I believe this method could lead to actual removal of cysts and tumors through the skin, without resorting to the use of instruments. This is similar or identical to some of the works done by some of the Philippine healers, sometimes called "psychic surgeons." Although there has been a lot of controversy about the reality of such operations, I am sure that such "miraculous" happenings are real and perfectly possible.

An energy *pull* can possibly be useful in a number of ways, such as stretching tendons and muscles without using physical force, or helping to free a pinched nerve in the spine. Just apply the energy with the intention that the pull will have the effect you wish to create. Your subject will, quite possibly, feel the pull in the area on which you are working. *Pushes* can be used where they would be effective in healing, as well.

SECTION 4.
Lifting The Spirit

Once you have worked with the healing energy, moving it around in various manners, you can also try what I call *lifting the spirit*. When a person's emotional tone is down in depression, fear, anger, or any other negative emotions, there is usually a downward flow of energy within the body. Therefore, if the healer can reverse this flow to an upward direction, the person's spirit will be lifted to a higher emotional level, at least for a while.

The ability to achieve this effect, or any other effect, is largely due to the decisions and intentions you put into the energy. I usually go through certain physical motions when I do this, but they are not really necessary. I hold my hands out, palms up, and I lift them a few inches, as I visualize the energy entering the body of the person to be "lifted," and traveling upward through his body, lifting his spirit to a higher level. Most people can feel this lifting effect, and most people can also do it effectively when they try. I can feel the energy I am moving, and you will probably feel it as well when you try it.

There are other ways to achieve the same effect. If I wish to do it without moving my hands, I can instead lift an energy flow upwards in my own body, and mentally push it into the other person, or simply intend that he feel it. Or, I will *be* the other person, and lift the energy in my body as though it were his, then be myself again. Or, I will just decide to lift the energy in his body, and visualize doing it. I usually use the hand motions, especially when I am teaching another person.

This can be done for a group of people simultaneously, with no difficulty. I was giving a talk on healing to a group of twenty people at a house church one evening, and I decided to demonstrate the lifting effect. As I led up to it, I thought, "Gee, I've never handled this many people at one time before. What if I can't do it?" Then the thought came that it is God's force, and that He could do it. I felt a terrific flow of energy as I lifted my hands. Almost everyone there felt the lift.

This effect can also be done at a distance. Try it.

SECTION 5.
Calming and Relaxing as an Aid in Reducing Blood Pressure

After I developed the above technique, I decided that I should be able to relax or calm a person by holding my hands up with the palms facing toward him, and settling the energy downward gently over him with the intention of calming him. I tried it, and it worked. This relaxes a person very quickly.

If you stop to think about it, this technique is a benediction, one that you can really feel.

Some time ago, at the Advanced Perception Class, I was giving healing to one of the students. As I finished, one of the graduate students said, "I'm next. My stomach is upset, and my chest is congested, too." After working on her chest for a couple of minutes, I held my hands with my palms toward her stomach. The effect was immediate. She told me she relaxed so quickly that she almost dropped to the floor.

Now, let us consider the end of a church service where the pastor or priest is giving the Benedictio; as he raises his arms in the traditional gesture. If he is at peace himself, and if he can project this energy of God's love to others with intentions of peace and calmness, he can leave the peace of God with his congregation in just this manner. How peaceful do YOU feel as your minister gives his Benediction? Is it only a ritual and a gesture with no effect, or can you feel the effect in your entire being?

After coming to the foregoing conclusions, I have since found some other healers are doing the same thing. Be sure to try this technique for helping to correct a disturbed digestive system.

This same technique is very useful in reducing blood pressure. It usually works quickly, and sometimes has the desired effect within just a few seconds. As you flow the relaxing energy, visualize it expanding the capillaries, with the pressure going down as a result. It would then be a good idea to teach the patient how to collect energy and do it for himself. People are being taught how to reduce their own blood pressure by means of biofeedback equipment, so why not teach them in this simple manner?

If you are a minister, I suggest that you consider the above possibilities carefully, and give this technique a try, for at least a few weeks. See if any of your congregation notices a difference. There should be some feedback to indicate the value of it. Let us put God's Power back into the Church, as well as into everyday living!

SECTION 6.
How to Control The
Emotional Vibrations Around You

Occasionally a person will ask, "What can I do about the person who is always radiating bad or negative vibes, and disturbing me so I can not do my work properly?" The bad vibes referred to may be negative emotions such as anger, confusion, hate, grief, etc. There

The Calming and Relaxing Technique
You can feel the energy being directed
toward you. Just make the decision to feel it!
(Instructions start on page 55.)

are several possible solutions to this problem, besides the common one of just suffering. Consider these alternatives:

a. Try to change the emotional level of the offender, as is described in "Lifting the Spirit" or "Calming and Relaxing."

b. Put up a psychic mirror that will reflect the offender's emotional flows back to him. This is quite simple to do. Just create with your mind the thought of a mirror between you, which is intended to reflect his vibes back to him. Be sure to project creative energy to it to give it more reality than just a casual thought.

This is NOT the best procedure to follow, as it will tend to intensify his negativity, even though you will be more comfortable. Some have imagined putting up a reflector or deflector to deflect the energy off to one side. If you try this, please don't deflect it so it is aimed at one of your friends, or he may not stay your friend for very long.

c. Decide to make yourself transparent to the emotions he is projecting. I call this the *clean window* effect, as this is a good description of the technique used. Remember, you can *always* choose the energy you wish to accept. Imagine or visualize that you are as transparent as a clean window to his emanations, and let his vibes pass right through you without being absorbed at all. It may take some practice to become proficient at this, but it will really pay off and give you greater peace of mind. It leaves you clean, without having to return his forces to him. They will then be returned to him according to the natural laws of the Universe, at the proper time.

One day the thought came to me that I could demonstrate the *clean window* effect to prove its worth, and so I did, to a young lady to whom I had been teaching some healing principles.

I said, "I'm going to radiate some discordant energy to you, like this, so you can feel it," and I proceeded to do so. She had an uneasy feeling as a result. "Now I want you to imagine yourself to be as transparent as a super clean window; let the energy simply flow through you." Then I repeated the discordant flow to her, but this time she could feel nothing; it went right through her. As I did it, *I* could tell that she could not feel it, as well. This demonstration proved to her that she did not have to accept the radiations, either good or bad, that another person puts out. It also showed me that the offender can tell when his radiations are not being accepted. It is similar to the situation of a radar signal going out, hitting a reflective object, and returning to be picked up by the receiving equipment, acknowledging that something is out there. If the object is now replaced with a non-reflecting one, there is no signal returned, with an entirely different result.

This means that if the offender is not getting the usual response from those around him, he may reach a point where he will stop radiating to such persons. Practicing with this should give you a greater ability to feel the way you want to feel.

It should be borne in mind that *nobody else makes you feel as you do.* You make yourself feel that way, by accepting what the other person is radiating to you. It does *not* have to be accepted if you don't want it, and are willing to *do* something about controlling your own area of responsibility.

    d. The most desirable way to handle it is to *convert* the anger (or any other negative emotion) to love, then send some of it back to the other person. This may sound impossible, but it can be done with a bit of practice, and it is *far* more valuable than the other ways of responding. How is it possible at all? Well, it must be possible; we are told in the sacred writings that we should love our enemies.

    If you are working with these healing energies, you have found that the same energy can be used in various ways, and it follows the thoughts put into it. It can be (and is) projected with either love or hate (or other emotions), to promote either excitement or calmness, disease or health, etc. This means that if you are receiving this energy in the form of negative vibrations, you can accept the energy itself as love, by changing it yourself, and then you will find it easy to return some of that love to the sender. You will find that you can demonstrate this technique as easily as the *clean window* effect. Try it with someone; don't take my word for it. If you try it, you will know that you can do it, and it will probably come in handy sometime, for you or someone else.

    Let me clarify this procedure. The change of vibrations, from negative to positive, comes from *your decision to change them;* in the same manner as you would decide, "I'm going to give Hank some healing to calm him," or "I'm flooding energy through Mary's muscles to wash out the fatigue," or any other use of this power. Your decision is what shapes the results. Just say to yourself, "I'm accepting these vibes as love," and feel them as love. I would suggest practicing this with a friend, in order to get this technique under control.

Mastering this method will actually give you control of the emotional vibrations surrounding you. No matter what others are experiencing, you will probably be able to change the emotions of those around you, provided they are ready to be helped.

SECTION 7.
Helping to Control Bleeding

This can be done by visualizing the flow of blood decreasing in a number of ways. One way is to visualize the blood vessels being completely intact and perfect. Another is to picture the cut or damaged vessels as shrinking, and the blood as clotting, thus cutting down the flow of blood. Or, visualize the damaged vessels being tied off. Or, visualize bandages being wrapped around the wound to produce the same effect. In the case of a hemorrhage, visualize it clearing up, leaving no residue to clog the system. *Do not ignore medical procedures!* Use these techniques only as an adjunct to proper medical treatment.

You may be able to detect and locate blood clots by passing your hand over the body, while your mind is focused only on the clots. You might be able to disperse and destroy them by visualizing them dissolving (not as just breaking up), and being gone from the system. Use the methods that seem best to you.

Some time ago, I was intending to visit one of my friends, but she called me and said that I should not come. She had just had a tooth pulled, and the bleeding was bothering her. I decided to alter that. The young lady had been a very good subject for hypnosis at choir parties where I had performed. I concentrated on her and gave her mental suggestions that the bleeding was reducing, as I visualized the capillaries shrinking, to cut down on the bleeding. I believe it was the next day when I heard that she was worried, because she had what in dentistry is called a "dry socket," where the bleeding stops, instead of draining slowly to get rid of the poisons. I had given my suggestions too well. I immediately gave suggestions to allow a cleansing flow of blood, which then occurred. I never confessed to the young lady, until much later, that I had been involved with what had happened at that time.

Since then, whenever I am assisting in healing a tooth extraction, I always visualize a certain amount of draining occurring to maximize healing. You do not have to know just how much drainage is necessary; just visualize with the feeling that everything is functioning as it should. God knows what the right amount is.

SECTION 8.
"Cleansing the Aura"

The *aura* is the life energy field surrounding the living body. Although it is normally invisible to most people under ordinary conditions, visual perception of it can be enhanced by certain lighting conditions, or by special training. Some people see it easily and naturally, without anyone else having told them such a thing exists. It is not an imaginary condition.

Some *see* the aura in colors, which indicate to them the physical and emotional state of the subject viewed. Internal problems are reflected in the external configuration and radiance of the aura, somewhat similar to a malfunctioning part of a machine, affecting the total sound pattern coming from the machine, thus leading to the detection and correction of the problems. There are even some psychics who obtain the information for their readings, from the aura of the person.

The meanings ascribed to the colors seen in the aura however, are not universal. That is, not all those who see the colors are in agreement as to the meaning of each color. It is much the same as our "feeling" the healing energy in various ways; such as a tingle, heat, cool breeze, pressure, and others. Each of us transforms it to a type of feeling that is acceptable to our own being.

I was attending a conference on spiritual matters, and was assigned to tape-record some of the various workshops. On one particular afternoon, I was assigned to record a workshop relating to the aura. A white sheet had been suspended vertically as a background, against which to better view the aura. The workshop leader would ask a volunteer to stand before the screen, then the aura colors would be observed, described, and explained. Special attention was drawn to any irregularities in the color of the aura, as well as to its clarity.

The workshop leader was showing her audience how to "cleanse the aura," then had one member of the audience use the technique on one of the others. Attention was drawn to the changes in the aura as the cleansing proceeded. In case you would like to try the process yourself, this is essentially the method she used.

You, as the healer, stand in front of the subject. Stoop down and extend your hands, as though you are going to reach under the feet of the subject. Visualize reaching to the aura under the feet, and cleansing or removing the "dirtiness" of the aura, as you bring your hands up along the sides of the subject. Continue to move them up the length of the subject's body, ending the action with both hands above the subject's head. Turn to one side, holding your hands as though they are full of the dirty energy that had been in the aura. Then mentally ask that the dirty energy be returned to the Source of all energy, for cleaning and recycling. Then wipe your hands on your clothes, as if to remove any residue. Repeat the cleansing passes for a total of four times, after which you are finished with the process. Check with the subject to find if any difference is felt as a result.

Now, after explaining the process, I would like for you to look closely at the entire situation. The aura is merely the radiation, or reflection, of the energy inside the subject, and is not an independent thing. In a sense, this "aura-cleansing" is approaching the problem in reverse! It works, of course, but let us put things in their proper perspective. The cause of the *dirty* areas and irregularities in the aura, is the misuse or imbalance of the energies inside the subject.

Therefore, it seems that a more direct way to put the aura into the proper condition, would be to channel pure healing energy to fill the subject's entire being. Channel this with loving thoughts of removing the negative and improper patterns and other hindrances, then see him in perfect energy balance, glowing with a strong, radiant aura. Don't worry about the old, dirty energy at all. It is automatically recycled every time, if you program, it by expecting it.

If you are in a healing group, you might set up a screen to help view the aura, and experiment for yourselves. It should be interesting, as well as instructive. Don't worry if there are those in your group who claim they do not see auras. Due to the "group effect," the perception of each one in the group will be higher than it is under ordinary conditions. Simply program your meeting at the start, with the prayer or thought of each member's perception being increased. This experience may tend to open new avenues of your perception. As I have mentioned before, the quickest way to safely increase any ability you have, is to make a dedication and commitment to be of help to others, and then apply it at every opportunity.

SECTION 9.
A Simple Back Technique

One Sunday evening, I attended a healing service conducted by some other healing channels, and I observed the following technique being used to benefit the spine. It should be emphasized that, although in this case the subjects were touched, the same effects can be produced without touching, at any distance.

Have the subject either sit on a stool, or sit sideways on a regular chair (unless you are doing it at a distance, of course). This gives freer access to the spine. You, as the healer, stand or kneel in back of the subject. Place your thumbs at the top of the subject's spine. Hold your thumbs about 1/2" to 3/4" apart at the tips. Do not apply pressure; just a gentle contact will do, or do not touch at all. Decide to flow energy to the spine, to remove tensions and imbalances, to improve alignment, and to allow free and healthy movement. After a couple of seconds or so, move the thumbs down to the next vertebra and repeat the process.

Use your intuition regarding the length of time to spend on each spot, or go by the amount of energy flowing. Energy flows according to the need for it. As the need is supplied, the flow decreases. Proceed in this manner all the way down the spine. You will probably find that it is very easy to detect the tense, injured or misaligned areas while doing this, as you feel a different feeling in your thumbs as you work on those specific vertebrae. This difference is usually felt as heat or a tingle, but not always; it may just be sensed as a different energy flow. It will be felt whether the subject has a lot of clothing over the area or not.

The subject can also feel that something is happening when your thumbs are applied to these disturbed spots. It, too, may be felt in a number of ways, but my experience has shown that it will be felt in some way, whether the subject has had awareness training or not.

Occasionally, you will find a subject who feels pain when you channel energy to the trouble spot. If so, just keep applying the energy to the area, and the pain will clear up. This will be the signal that the application for that area is sufficient; move on. When finished, have the subject claim the healing by testing the mobility of the spine, if practical to do so.

Alternate methods may be used to achieve the

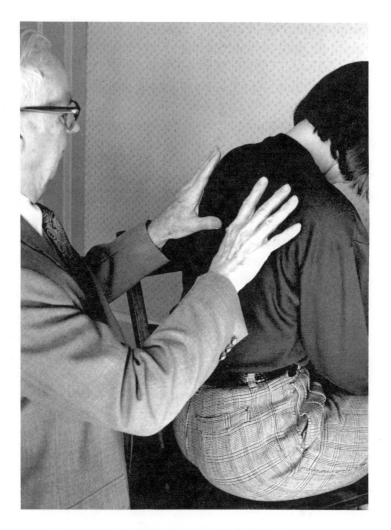

A SIMPLE BACK TECHNIQUE
Thumb tips are approximately $^3/_4$ inch apart.
(Instructions start on page 67.)

same effect. For example, you may be sitting next to a person in need of healing, and it may be awkward or inconvenient to use the position described. In such a case, use the thumb and finger of one hand to do the same thing, instead of using the thumbs of both hands. Remember, thought controls energy; *it is not what you are doing physically that is important, but what your mind is doing.*

If you are one of those hard-core skeptics who is just reading this book to see what sort of hogwash this author is putting out, then I challenge you to try these techniques! There are so many people with back problems, that you can easily find someone to try it on. But please try to set aside your negative thoughts while you do it.

You will find that this is a very simple and effective technique, that is easily shown, and easily grasped. It is ideal to teach to husbands and wives to use on each other. Just about everyone to whom I have shown it has been able to use it, and also to feel its' effectiveness.

SECTION 10.
Increasing Your Rapport with Another
- Mending Relationships -

This technique could very well be the most important one in this book. Increasing your rapport with the person you are trying to heal is certainly desirable. It also helps you to become more in tune with the Universe around you.

Get a friend, or even a stranger, to join with you.

Both of you hold your hands out in front of you with the palms up. Each one decides to accept only pure energy from God, and wills that energy to go to the other. After you have done this for only about five seconds, you will feel an increased attraction or closeness for each other! You see, *the pure energy is LOVE! God is Love!*

To use as a healing method for a disturbed relationship, picture the other person in front of you, holding his or her hands as instructed above. Hold yours similarly. As you channel the pure energy to that person, if you feel the response of love or the increased closeness, you know that you have reached him or her. The next time you talk to that person, the increased rapport will probably be evident. This is because every soul is always aware, on some level, of everything that is happening; even aware that you are, at that moment, sending your love! Try it. It works, and fast!

After you have tried this method, try the following for a more intense flow of ecstatic energy.

This is a contact technique. Have the other person and yourself sit facing each other, palms up, and touch each other's fingers; your right hand to his left, and vice versa. Now, decide to flow that pure energy back and forth, simultaneously. Note how the rapport builds higher and higher, to an ecstatic level! It is really a great experience, as you will find. Look into each other's eyes as you do it.

Be sure to clear yourself by wiping the hands together, as shown previously, when you are through.

If you should ever feel lonely or unloved, and you are a Christian, just visualize Jesus in front of you and channel to Him, and you will feel the love return immediately. Or, do it with any of the saints, or Buddha, or any other elevated being, and KNOW that he or she loves you! *YOU are the only one who can keep anyone's love from you!*

SECTION 11.
Raising the Christ Consciousness

The great psychic, Edgar Cayce, gave much information on being a channel for healing. He stated that, in order to truly heal, you must raise the *Christ Consciousness* of the person in need of healing, and also your own. Therefore, when I am doing healing, I visualize the subject opening the barriers to his own super-consciousness, or Christ Consciousness. This does not mean that the subject has to be of the Christian faith (healings occur in all religions, and even without religion), as this is a very limited view of religious interpretation. The Christ Consciousness is that part of us all which is in contact with God. A whole person, one who is totally integrated, has unified the conscious, the subconscious, and the super-conscious minds. "Holy" means "wholly." A "whole" person is one who has removed the limitations he has erected in the past, and knows who he is, where he has been, and where he is going.

Do not confuse the man Jesus with the concept "Christ," which means "Annointed." *Christ* means that He had attained knowledge of His relation to God, as He said, "The Father and I are One," meaning reunited. "It is not I who doeth these things, but the Father within me."

Remember the picture showing the Christ knocking at the door? There is no latch on the outside of the door, indicating that you must open the door to allow the Christ to enter into your consciousness. Therefore, to assist in healing a person, visualize him opening the door to his Christ Consciousness, and allowing the Christ Power within him to heal his body. *The healing energy IS the Christ Power.*

This does not mean that Christians are the only ones who can contact the Christ Consciousness, as *all of us* have that inner "Light" or "Way" to God, regardless of the name we assign to it, and regardless of our religious affiliation or lack of it. Bear in mind the fact that people of all religious persuasions (and atheists, too) receive healings, both the standard type and the miraculous type. In any healing, fast or slow, the same forces must be present for it to occur.

There is an energy *pattern body* that the physical body follows in its growth. In healing, we must reach this pattern body, and try to change it with our thoughts and energy, visualizing the perfection that we wish to see materialized. In some of the Cayce material, we are told that this healing energy tends to tune or align the molecules of the body, and the forces of the mind, to allow the healing to take place.

As our weekly healing classes have progressed, we have found it important to address the innermost consciousness of the subject in order to best initiate healing changes. How do you do this? By simply directing your healing thoughts with that purpose in mind, visualizing those thoughts going to the higher consciousness. Remember that this inner consciousness created the illness in the first place, so it also has the power to heal. Perhaps it can be persuaded to recreate health. Talk to it. Tell it to learn the lesson to be learned, so it can create a healthy mind and body again.

SECTION 12.
The Use Of Water in Healing

One day I was experimenting with my ENERGY WHEEL®, which is a sensitive psychic motor of my own design and construction. I had been practicing with it and was moving it quite easily, by putting my hands around it and directing the energy to it. I knew that there would be some people who would blame the motion of the rotor on static electricity in the body. I rubbed my finger on my pants to increase any such charge on the finger, and brought it near the rotor to see if there was a perceptible charge. There was no effect on the rotor. Then I reasoned that if there were such a charge, wetting my fingertip with my tongue would drain the charge from my finger. I wet my finger and brought it near the rotor, and the rotor jumped in response, quite the opposite of what I had expected. I repeated the experiment. Adding the saliva increased the energy flow. I discovered that if there is no motion observed when you first wet the finger, it will build up much more strongly if you repeat the wetting. Evidently, your intention to build up the charge of energy causes just that to happen.

At the time, I analyzed the foregoing as follows:

a. The healing energy acts, in some ways, in a manner similar to electricity.

b. Water is usually an aid to the conductivity of

electricity, except for pure water, which is an insulator.

c. If the fingers are wet, it should therefore be easier to transmit energy to another person.

The test of this came only a few minutes later, when one of my friends called me on the phone to ask for healing for her back. I pictured her in front of me, located the area of the disturbance, and started to channel energy to her. I had a sudden thought. I said, "Wait a minute; I want to try something." I went to the washtub a few feet away and wet my hands, then returned to the phone, and again started to give her healing. "How does that feel?" I asked. "Wow! What did you do? How did you do that?" was her response. She said there was a great increase in the energy when my hands were wet. Since then, we have had other healers wet the hands, with similar results.

It doesn't seem to matter whether it is a contact healing or an absent healing; the transmission is increased in both cases. My explanation of the phenomenon, however, has changed; I see it now as an impedance-matching process. Here is my technical explanation.

In any energy-carrying system, if there are sudden changes in the impedance of the medium carrying the energy, there are reflections and losses produced. Maximum efficiency is attained when the impedance of the source or energy supply is equal to the impedance of the sink (where the energy goes). In electrical circuits, when changing from one impedance to another, the proper impedance-matching system must be used, to prevent energy loss or reflection. Your TV antenna is matched to the 300-ohm transmission line; this in turn is matched to the TV set's input circuitry. Any abrupt discontinuity or change must be modified or softened to permit the maximum amount of radio energy to be utilized by the set. The change must be gradual. In microwave transmission through a metal tube or wave guide, a funnel-shaped chamber must be used to transfer the waves without loss from one guide to either a larger or smaller guide.

In the field of acoustics or music, the principle is the same. The clarinet is a constant-bore instrument, and the saxophone is a tapered-bore instrument. In order to get the frequencies inside the tubing out into the room without distortion, the tubing must be expanded into a funnel shape, or the bell of the instrument. There is also a modification of shape at the other end. Observe how the tubing narrows down to match the impedance of the lips-and-reed combination. A trumpet, or any other brass instrument, has a similar impedance-matching funnel at each end. The funnel shape avoids a sharp (pun intended) transition, thus approaching the proper impedance gradually. A number of other examples in other fields could be cited.

Now, let us consider the following healing situation. In the energy flow from my fingers to yours, we have a sudden discontinuity in the medium carrying the energy: that is, my "solid" fingers, then the atmospheric gases, then your solid fingers, so that there is a double change. What changes occur when I wet my fingers and send energy in the same way? In doing so, we have interposed an intermediate form of matter, a liquid, between the solid-to-gas stage. An added feature of the liquid is that it evaporates into a gas, as well, thus softening the change still more. If you also wet your hands, still more energy will be received. You can easily check this by experiment.

One of my friends has noted that hot water has a greater effect than cold water, which is to be expected if the evaporation of the water is a factor. Another one of my psychic friends has told me that she is more sensitive to psychic impressions when she gets out of the bathtub, and since her whole body is wet.

Baptism

When you associate this phenomenon with the history of baptism using water, you can understand that most ministers and priests *do not know what they are supposed to be doing* during a baptism. The water, as such, means little: It is what the mind is doing during the ceremony that is important. A minister who knows about and uses the healing energy should be able to perform a much more effective and meaningful baptism. He could consciously project the healing energy with the intention to raise the consciousness of the baptized person to a higher level closer to the Christ Consciousness. If you are a minister, you might ask, "How will I know if this procedure will have such an effect?" The answer lies in trying it. Experiment with a sensitive adult who is a friend of yours, or a child who will cooperate. Children are usually quite sensitive. Conduct some experimental baptismal ceremonies both with and without using these techniques, and find out how the baptized person feels about each of the methods. The effect should be greater with a group of people present, especially if they know what you are trying to do and add their efforts to yours, channeling their power through you.

Jesus said, "I baptize you with *living water*." And the water used in baptism can be easily charged with this life energy, so that it can certainly be termed living water. Could this be what He referred to? I am inclined to believe so. The ancients annointed the heads of persons with oils when they laid on hands for healing. Some still do it today. I believe the real purpose was to increase contact with the flesh, and thus increase the energy flow. Of course, an oil will not evaporate as rapidly as water from your hands, so it will last longer. It is my opinion that the oil will not be as effective as water for aiding absent healing, but only for contact healing. One reason that water is so effective is that water is an extension of the flesh itself, since the body is composed of mostly water.

SECTION 13.
Feeling and Healing
the Inner Organs

Since the space between our healing hands and the patient is in effect negated, it is possible to "hold" a malfunctioning inner organ between our hands (in our minds), to fill it with white light and see it functioning perfectly.

One day a friend and I were talking about Father

N., a priest who was in the hospital at the time. She mentioned that he was having a lot of trouble breathing. I had a sudden inspiration. I said, "Let's try something. Imagine that we are reaching inside his body and holding his lungs between our hands, and flow a white light between them to permeate the lungs. We will move our hands first together, then apart, and visualize his lungs following this expansion and contraction, cleansing them, and see the breathing going back to normal."

She did as I did, and then said with some surprise, "Gerry, I can actually feel his lungs!" Later she reported to me that the doctors were amazed at the improvement in his breathing.

Occasionally, I have used this same idea to help heal other organs, such as heart, liver, pancreas, etc. It is a useful and interesting technique -- try it. Incidentally, it is also possible that the patient will feel it happening within his body.

SECTION 14.
The Subconscious
Self-Examination System

This Subconscious Examination therapy is very useful and powerful for doing certain types of healing. It has been used by many people for many years in a number of ways, I am sure, but I learned of it comparatively recently.

I was in the process of copying some lecture tapes for the library of the Spiritual Frontiers Fellowship, whose offices were then located in Evanston, Illinois.

One tape I listened to as I copied was a talk on "How to Heal Using the Subconscious Suggestion Principle," given by Louise Eggleston at Charlotte, N.C., on October 30, 1970. In this talk, she told of some wonderful healings of people near death, achieved by talking to them while they were in a coma. Other healings involved talking to an ill person while he is asleep, or talking to him while out of his hearing, in case he is awake. I saw great value in this system, but I also saw how it could be modified to be of use for a number of things other than those mentioned in the lecture. Louise Eggleston said that this technique, when properly used, is ten times more powerful than a prayer group, and I believe she is right.

As I recall, the technique, as she presented it in her talk, was used on a dying person in a coma, for example, in the following manner. Members of the patient's family or friends, and sometimes nurses, were to take turns in talking out loud to him every hour. Someone was to always be there and reading or speaking essentially the following suggestions:

(First, the person is called by name three times) "--, you will listen closely to what I say. You are wanted and needed by your family and friends. God has some important work for you to do. You want to do His will. Christ is healing, renewing your body and mind, even now. Your work on earth is not yet finished," and so on. This was only done in the person's presence when he was unconscious, and at other times at a distance when he was asleep.

According to my own evaluations of it after adding personal modifications, its greatest value is in breaking a person out of a stuck pattern condition. The stuck person is in a pattern rut, but he usually does not realize it. He does not know how to get out of the pattern, even if he should become aware of it. It is usually ineffective to tell him about his condition, because he is unable to listen and talk intelligently about it. His emotional pattern is such that it takes over instead, and you simply cannot get through to him by talking. External advice is just turned off, and has no effect.

The beautiful part of this system is that not a word of the technique is said to the person on a conscious hearing level in his presence. Most of us are aware that it is less than effective to tell such a stuck person as an alcoholic, for example, that he is harming himself and others, that he should stop it, that he is wasting his life, etc. The spoken words are turned off, rejected by the person. The self-evaluation and the decision to change *must come from within him,* or any change will not be permanent. This method is a way of sneaking in through the back door, so to speak, so that the ideas and suggestions come up from his subconscious mind as his own ideas, even though they were put there by your suggestions.

Direct Mental Suggestion

Direct mental suggestions could be used to force a person to change, to a certain degree, but the use of such force must be avoided, for your own protection. Make no mistake about it, all forces must balance in this universe, and if you apply such a force it will return to you in like manner. If you apply any force to make another person do something he does not want to do, the time will come when the same force will be used on you.

If the stuck person could see himself exactly as others see him, or as he really is, he would most likely decide to change and get out of his rut. Therefore, notice that we do not apply the suggestions to *make* him change, but only to cause him to look at himself and *see himself accurately*. Use this technique daily on such a person for a period of two weeks or so. The repeated discomfort of seeing himself and what he has done to himself and others, plus realizing what progress can be made in himself and his relationships with those around him, usually will be sufficient to make him decide he would be more comfortable if he were to make some needed changes.

Of course, this technique sounds totally unbelievable to many people, but don't let that stop you from trying it on someone who needs help. Remember, the only valid criterion for any technique is whether it works and does what it is designed to do, regardless of theories to the contrary.

Louise Eggleston said, "You often hear from the subject's mouth the very words you have implanted in his mind." I have had this verified by a statement from a young man some time after I had been using the technique on him. I was giving him instructions in using the system in order that he might use it on another person. As I explained the part about pulling up the thoughts like pulling weeds from a garden, he said,

"You know, I was doing that same thing some time ago." I replied, "I know you were, because I included that same phrase when I used it on you over a year ago."

A similar result was achieved by one of the students attending my class in Spiritual Healing. She told us that her daughter was an alcoholic, had left home, and never kept in touch. She mentioned that she wished she knew how she could be of help, so I gave her a copy of the technique to use. In the mental suggestions, she told her daughter to look into the visualized mirror and see her *real* Self. The next month when she was back with us, she told us, "Well, it worked! It's hard to believe, but it worked. My daughter called me, and said that she had been looking in the mirror and seeing herself for the first time, and was ready to change."

One day some friends brought a friend of theirs over for a Tarot reading. Her husband had lost his job, and he was afraid to go out and look for another one, for fear of failing. He also had a physical problem, and was in need of healing. I started to apply the technique to him, and was channeling healing to him through his wife. Then I decided that she should be using it on him, so I taught her to use the technique. She started to apply it. The next time I stopped in to see her at the drug store where she worked, she said, "For the first time, my husband got out his tools and fixed something in the house without being asked!" The next time I saw her, she told me he had a new job.

The technique is intended to take effect while the subject is sleeping or otherwise receptive, while the conscious mind is out of the way. It does not matter whether the person is close by or at a great distance. The subconscious mind works without the space and time limitations of the conscious mind. While we are sleeping we dream of the past, present and future equally easily. Read, *An Experiment With Time* by J. W. Dunne. The important point is that if the patient is in another city, or another part of the world, you do not have to use the technique only when he is asleep. You can pick a time convenient for yourself, and have the method take effect while the subject is asleep. This is done simply by saying to yourself, when you are starting the process, "The following suggestions are to be applied when ---- (the subject) is asleep and receptive." Your subconscious will then transmit the information at a time when the subject's subconscious is receptive and the conscious mind is inactive, usually during sleep.

Nine Phase Healing Process

We will refer to the person who is being worked on as the patient, inasmuch as this is a healing process; we will refer to the one who is doing the process as the operator.

As I examine the Process as I have revised it, it seems it should be composed of or considered as nine phases:

1. The patient is asked to examine his old decisions, goals, attitudes, actions and reactions.

2. He is asked to judge the above material, to see if it is up-to-date, or outmoded and no longer serving the best interests of the patient and those around him.

3. He is asked to view himself as he really is, and asked if this is the person he was sent here to be. It is then suggested that he is able to see the future as he is now headed.

4. He is given a view of the possibilities of the future if he makes some changes. For example, attaining the soul's purpose in being here, seeing himself happier and relating to others on a higher level, loving and being loved, being closer to God, etc.

5. He is asked to consider forgiving others for anything done to him in the past, ask others to forgive him in a like manner, and to accept forgiveness --- this is very important --- in order to remove barriers to his own development.

6. He is asked to examine past traumatic events for the lessons they contain, in order to prevent future repetitions.

7. The patient is assured of support and healing energy from those around him, to achieve the desired changes.

8. The decision to change or stay the same should always be left up to the patient.

9. You, as the operator, should expect it to work. See the patient changing, in your mind. Be persistent.

Mental Healing Session

We will now go through a typical session, just as I would use it on such a stuck person. We will call him "Archie Kenway" for convenience.

First, I get into a comfortable position, and

breathe deeply a few times, to relax more fully. I also turn my palms upward to take in extra energy. Then I say to myself, "The following is to be applied to Archie when he is asleep and receptive." I now visualize Archie before me, if I know him. If I don't know him, I address the name only, realizing that God knows him, and that he will get the message anyway. *"Archie Kenway! Archie Kenway! Archie Kenway!* (I call three times). *Are you listening?* (visualize him answering yes, or nodding his head). *Archie, you are going to examine yourself very carefully on all levels. You will examine your decision structure: all your decisions, both verbalized and felt decisions, to see if they should still apply to today's and tomorrow's living, and consider the possibility of changing those which no longer fit the situations now present and those coming up. You will examine your attitudes, toward yourself and those around you, and see if some of these attitudes should be brought up to date for a better future. You will examine closely the goals you have set at various times, and see if these should be revised in view of today's situations. You will examine your actions and reactions with others around you, and decide which of these should be changed for a better future. You are going to consider forgiving others for everything they have done to you in the past, since you are now realizing that we are forgiven in accordance with our willingness to forgive others. This will help you to overcome barriers to your own development.*

(Now picture a mirror in front of him, to one side). *"Now look into this mirror. It shows you as you really are, and not the way you usually consider yourself to be. Is this the person you intended to be when you came on this earth? Is this the person God intended you to be, when He sent you here?* (See him being startled at what he sees). *Look again into the mirror, as it also shows you where your present patterns are taking you, unless you make some changes that you know should be made.* (Picture the mirror being replaced by another one, on the other side). *Now look into this other mirror, which shows you the greater person you could be, and will be if you make certain changes within yourself. See the increased helpfulness, both in giving and receiving. See the greater happiness you would give and receive. See the increased closeness to God you would experience. See yourself attaining your purpose in being here on earth. See yourself breaking down the barriers to your progress, and pushing back the limitations to your abilities. This is the great, loving and loved person you will be, if you make those changes. You know the changes that have to be made to achieve this. You will get all the energy and help you need from God and those around you to make those changes. You will see the automatic patterns that you have been using, and you will see the means of breaking those patterns you decide are no longer desirable.*

"You will not condemn yourself for your past errors, but instead consider doing something to rectify your actions in the future. You will dig up, from deep in your mind, the traumatic things that disturb you; as you would pull up weeds by the root from a garden. You will examine these things closely, and extract the lesson that was to be learned from each, as they are illumined by God's light, and then discard them as the trash they are. (Picture him doing just that). *You will then be free of their influence. You will examine the "bad" things that have happened to you, study their emotional content and learn the things you were sup-*

posed to learn from each experience, then let them lie, unable to affect you any more. Your fears and failures will no longer bother you, but you will look to the future and create a new you, the real you, and you will thank the Lord for having seen yourself and having achieved the growth."

I then visualize Archie as having already made the needed changes, and thanking the Lord, and I thank the Lord as well, for the changes that are to take place. I cut off the flow of healing energy at this point, and release the whole works by thinking of something else.

Please note that you do not force the person to make any changes --- you just ask him to look at himself. If you do use this system (or any other system, for that matter) to force a person to do something, you are the one who will have to suffer, when the same force is later used on you as it must be. All forces in the Universe must balance! Therefore, it is best just to use the suggestions to look at the self.

The suggestions given in this manner come up from the subconscious mind of the patient when he is awake, as though they are his own thoughts, and they are therefore harder to ignore than words from concerned friends, heard with the ears. Such words merely serve to activate a defensive mechanism, in which the patient must maintain his stand, and tends to keep him on the same path. Do not suggest to him that he is doing anything wrong, as you would then be judging him. He is the one who has all the pertinent data within himself, and he is the one who must judge himself, to correct his aim.

The Irritation Factor

When the suggestions to see himself surface to his outer conscious, as a result of using this technique, it is more than likely that he will become somewhat irritable (or more irritable than usual), as he *really* sees the self he has created. Use caution here: play it cool, and keep your emotions (and your tongue), under control to avoid undoing what you have done on the inner levels.

This irritation factor can be used as an indicator that the technique is working, particularly if you are in daily contact with the subject. Once you see the irritation manifesting, add the following suggestion to the other suggestions given: "*As you become irritated and dissatisfied with yourself as you are now, you will realize that this is your problem alone, one that you have to resolve, and that you cannot blame it on anyone else. Therefore, you will not direct this irritation toward those around you, but you will keep it within yourself, where it belongs.*" This should hasten the patient's desire to change, and make it easier on those around him. The changes in him will come when he becomes uncomfortable enough to say to himself, "I must do something about myself! I can't stand myself any more, the way I am. I've got to change something!" So the option to change is entirely his.

Sometimes the patient will be ready to change right away. With others, it will take persistence. If there are no perceptible results after using the system for a couple of weeks, I would recommend that you let up for a week, and then start afresh. If there are still no results, recheck your own motives and your own judgment.

Perhaps you are the one who is in error.

Here's a good example of the irritation factor. Recently, a friend of ours had been going with a certain man for quite some time. It seems that this man, although physically mature, is still tied quite strongly to his mother, who is apparently quite possessive. Our friend wanted to have him decide whether he wants to marry her, so I gave her this technique to use on him to see if it would help him make up his mind. I told her I would use the system on him as well.

About a week later, as I was on my way to her house to return an item we had borrowed, I thought that I had better point out to her the possibility of his becoming irritable. When I got to her house, the first thing she said was, "You had better let up on him a little, Gerry, as he's becoming quite irritable." I told her to keep it up, but without trying to push it, as the irritability is a sure sign that he is receiving the message. At that time, I had not yet thought of using the additional suggestions to control the irritability.

When the relationship between the operator and the patient is quite close, the operator may have to keep on using the system longer than otherwise, as the operator, in such a case, is usually part of the problem. It seems as if the operator's willingness to persist is being tested. Remember, the returns in growth are well worth the time and effort spent in using this technique.

Each person is creating his or her future at all times. If something goes wrong for you, look for the cause to be within you, and not someone else. For this reason, when one person is mistreating another who then comes to you for help, it is important that both parties receive the Examination System treatment, instead of only the one who is doing the mistreating. The other person is *drawing* the mistreatment to himself, in some manner.

When someone comes to me and says, "My husband (or wife) is mistreating me," I give the client the information on using this System, and agree to help by using the System myself, on the spouse. I also use the Self Examination System on the client, because no such problem is one-sided.

If something bugs you, you can bet that there is something within yourself that has invited the bugging; it shows that there is a need for improvement in that area of your development. The aim of anyone doing counseling should be to break *both* partners out of their patterns, to allow a better relationship to develop.

Occasionally a client will ask, "Can I also use this technique on myself?" Of course you can. Use it the same as you would autosuggestion. Get yourself relaxed and then give the suggestions to your own subconscious mind. You will probably notice an increase of old incidents popping into your mind for reexamination.

When a marriage breaks up, there are generally many unresolved emotional attitudes toward each other that both parties need to work out and overcome. Sometimes one of these "parted parties" will come to me for a reading concerning a new romantic venture with a new partner, and the Tarot cards indicate that the future relationship will be affected by the decisions and unresolved elements from the past married life. This indicates that the client should review past trauma in detail. One can uncover emotional decisions and other feelings to see what limits were set up at those times, and to extract the good or lesson which is somewhere in each such incident. This is one way to become free of those limiting times.

Resolving Past Trauma

What type of decision might be contained in one of those past traumatic situations? It might be a feeling, for example, that "I'll always have trouble with him (her) this way," or "I'm never going to change," or "I'll never meet the right one for me." Or it can be any other decision (which always contains emotion) which could serve to hold a person in a pattern from which it would be difficult to escape, especially with the "always" or "never" component present. When the original incident happened, it was probably forgotten, but the emotion present held it in place, to be reactivated or replayed whenever a similar situation presents itself.

Frequently the entire pattern is followed when triggered, without the person realizing that it is an automatic pattern. It functions similarly to of a post-hypnotic suggestion. The subject carries out the suggestions given by the hypnotist when the proper clue is given, without being aware that he is doing the action due to another person's direction. Look around you, and study the patterns your friends and family are following, without being aware of it. What patterns are you following without realizing it?

To defuse the pattern, go back and look at the emotions that were present the first time the it was used. Bring it up to full consciousness for examination. The re-experiencing and re-examination of the entire incident, including all emotions present, should free the energy locked there. This enables you to make some new decisions allowing you more suitable choices for the future, without having to follow a pattern of failure and frustration.

It is important to keep in mind that not all decisions are expressed in verbally-organized thoughts. Some are just feelings, but they are just as effective in holding us in patterns as those formed into words, either mental or actually spoken.

If the client's past spouse has a problem with a stuck pattern (which may have been an important factor in their parting), I usually recommend that the client use this Self Evaluation System on the former spouse, just for the purpose of helping another human being who is in need of help. This is especially important when there are bad feelings between them, and when the client wants to have nothing more to do with the former partner.

If the System is used in this manner, with such a purpose, in mind, the client cannot help but benefit from having given time and effort to help someone who no longer means much to him. It probably helps to cut down some of the karmic obligations of the user or operator toward the subject. (Karmic obligations are those carried over from a past life to the present one.) Besides, the mental processes exercised in using this System build up a better rapport with the user's subconscious mind.

When you are emotionally involved with the patient on whom the System is being used, it is important to keep your emotions in control during the times that you are using the technique. If you are projecting your usual feelings at such a time, the patient will automatically tend to return his usual emotions in a like manner, and will be less inclined to accept the suggested idea as his own thoughts. Another important factor --- don't tell him, when you are using the technique, what *you* believe he is doing wrong. Just tell him to look at what he is doing, and that is sufficient. Otherwise you would be judging him. The inner self knows whether any action is right or wrong for his development, without any outside help.

If more than one person is using the technique on the same patient, it is very important that the operators agree on what suggestions to use, to avoid confusion due to conflicting suggestions.

This Technique should be very useful in the rehabilitation of criminals who keep returning to crime, to help them break their patterns. It should also be useful to the members of an alcoholic's family. It is probably a good idea to use it on the rest of the family, as well as on the alcoholic, since in most cases the family, or some aspect of it, is part of the problem. You should cover all possibilities in trying to solve a problem such as this.

A percentage of readers are likely to be shocked at the idea of giving hypnotic suggestion, and will cry out, "But you are manipulating the patient, without his consent!" The fact is that every person *always* has the option of accepting or rejecting any suggestion that is made, whether it is under normal consciousness, hypnosis, drugs, or any other method or condition. The soul is always aware, and is always in control. Man's free will can never be bypassed. We are given free will by God, and we always have it. If it sometimes seems as though we no longer have it, we are not looking deep enough. Our inner self has made the agreement to get us into this mess in which we find ourselves, in order that we may grow as we work our way out of it. Keep this in mind. *Manipulation is always by consent*, at some level of the person's being.

Therefore, do not be afraid of using the Subconscious Examination System on a person who needs help. If that person is not ready to be helped, the suggestions simply will not be accepted. Each suggestion you give to that person will be accepted or rejected according to what that soul needs from *his* viewpoint, not yours.

Remember, that the intention behind the suggestion is important. You are responsible for the intentions you have toward all persons. If your intention is to make the other person change because you think he should change, that intention will cause the same force to be applied to you at some time. If your intention is to bring healing, to provide a clue or means by which he can heal himself, the suggestions will have a much better chance of achieving their goal, and only good can return to you as a result.

SECTION 15.
"Responsibility" Problem-Solving

One of the most difficult things to learn, is that each person is the author of his own book of life, whether it be a book of tragedy, comedy, mystery, or a book of blank pages. There is a saying that every time you point a finger blaming someone else for something done to you, there are three fingers pointing back at you. The phenomenon of projection is well known, whereby a person is easily able to see in another the very faults that are within himself. Like a radio, we *tune in* to another's faults because we have a broadcasting station within, which is tuned to that same frequency.

One of the keys to our own development, therefore, is the study of our own reactions to the people with whom we associate, those we meet, and especially those with whom we would NOT associate, as these people are similar to parts of ourselves which need resolution and healing.

We are the source of our own problems, no matter what kind of problems they are. The Universe is ONE unit, ONE force, made by ONE GOD. Everything is in its rightful place, and the Universe is so organized that its components will work together to bring each of us exactly the kind of problems we need for our development, and also the blessings that we allow ourselves to receive. One of the things that the great psychic Edgar Cayce said stands out in my mind, and it should merit deep thought and meditation. He said, in effect, that *a man can't possibly get into more trouble than he deserves.*

If the foregoing is true, the sooner that one realizes that he has created his difficulty for his own development, the sooner he will confront it and resolve it. If the cause is within him, the solution is also there. Sometimes if a person is willing to admit that he may have caused his own problem, the problem will ease up and disappear, as if it were created specifically for self-illumination. Having achieved its purpose, it then disappears.

Some people have great success in getting answers to problems through meditation. Others get them through remembering, recording, and interpreting their dreams. My approach in counseling others is to help them to see and plan where they are going, so they will need less outside assistance.

As a person becomes more spiritually developed, as he gets rid of more of his prejudices and emotional "hang-ups," he should be able to see more clearly where any contemplated action would take him. This enables him to make wiser choices, and thus cut down on the frictions involved with everyday living. He will then see more clearly that nobody else "did it" to him. That, in reality, he did it to himself, through his attitudes and decisions.

In 1969, I was thinking of the trouble that some people get into occasionally through the use of hypnosis, such as a case where the hypnotist gives suggestions to a subject, which results in a lawsuit against the hypnotist. This does not happen very often, but it has been known to happen. In thinking over this sort of occurrence, I reached a breakthrough in my understanding about responsibility and the interrelationships of people. I wrote down my conclusions on a piece of paper, and made several copies. Most of the other hypnotists I showed it to did not understand the principles involved, and so disagreed with me. Now, however, I am more certain than ever that my postulation is true. It reads as follows:

POSTULATION:
A Person Can Do No Harm
with Hypnosis

1. The cooperation or opposition between persons is due to the *super-conscious* relation or communication between all individuals, which exists in order to fulfill karmic obligations with or between others, thus providing the situations which can lead to spiritual progress when properly resolved.

2. Suppose a person must be put into a particular distressing situation by another, for resolution of some deficiency in their personality, as a step in development. On *some* level, then, the other person's super-conscious mind must agree to act as the precipitating agent, or channel.

3. If, therefore, a hypnotist gives an adverse suggestion to a subject which seems to cause trouble for either the subject or the hypnotist, or both, this can only happen when there is an agreement on some level that this conflict should happen.

4. If the above is true, then such "accidents" are

not accidents, but are agreed upon by both hypnotist and subject. Furthermore, they act as developmental opportunities for either or both parties.

5. A hypnotist who is aware of the above relationships and possibilities will seldom precipitate any of these accidents, if he decides firmly that he will not participate in them in that manner, that his sole (and soul) purpose is to help, and if he is in pretty good control over his area of living.

It further dawned on me that if this were true, one should take another look at other so-called accidents as well, such as automobile accidents where other persons are involved. Driving with these things in mind, and maintaining the proper attitudes toward self and others, would drastically alter the statistics of traffic accidents.

As a result of meditating on these ideas, I have come to use the following pattern for my driving, which I consider to be the safest one possible.

I make the decision that I will be in God's master safe traffic pattern at all times, for the maximum safety of motorists and pedestrians alike, knowing when I should take advantage and when I should not. I try to avoid condemning what another driver is doing, as I realize that he is creating his own reality as I am creating mine, and that the emotions I put out will come back to me. The things that he does to others will come back to him. I am responsible only for what happens to me.

Thus, it might be a good idea to go over in your mind the types of situations you would like to be responsible for helping to create, or participate in with others, whether you know those people now or not. This will probably help your inner self to lead you into actually experiencing these desirable situations. *Learn to expect good things to happen!*

SECTION 16.
The Harmony Room

This is one of the most useful healing techniques. One of our prime purposes here on earth seems to be to get along peacefully with other people, and most of us fall somewhat short in this area, at least once in a while. The person who gets along smoothly with everybody is rare.

The origin of this technique was in a dream I had one morning in March 1973, while in the process of waking. I knew my thoughts were connected with a problem-solving technique, so I wrote down the essence of the dream: "Create a system or place whereby, when several are involved in differences, you may call those who are ready to listen to a particular place or condition where they can see their own state, and change." As you can see, this was not very illuminating at the time, but I figured it had to be of importance.

Two months later, while attending one of the lectures at the Spiritual Frontiers Fellowship Conference in May, I was telling the young lady sitting next to me about the dream, when the rest of the system crystallized, so to speak, and I knew how to apply it. Here it is in its present form.

Create in your mind a compartment or room, which you will call your "Harmony Room." Create this with your ability to visualize or imagine things, to the best of your ability. If you do not have a vivid imagination or cannot make clear mental pictures, don't worry about it. Do the best you can. Just get a mental concept as clear as you can, and work with that. Your visualization will improve the more you use any of these techniques, since we are using Creative Energy in all of them.

Decide that anyone you put in that room must harmonize with you. If you have a good mind for details, you can furnish the room with your ideas of what such a harmony room would contain if actually constructed on the physical plane, such as furniture, pictures, flowers, color scheme, incense, music, etc. Each additional detail adds to the creative energy, and therefore to its' reality, due to the intention put there. I repeat: You do not have to have the ability to see it in your mind as an actual picture. As long as you have a mental concept of such a room, and expect it to work, it will be just fine. (Some friends of mine, who have been blind since birth, use visualization very effectively.)

Once you have the room constructed in your mind, visualize it being filled with healing energy as pure harmony. Draw in energy, and see it filling your Harmony Room to overflowing. When you feel that this is accomplished, put the image or concept of the person with whom you are having relationship difficulties into the room, with the intention that the person will now be filled with the harmonious vibrations in the room. See him becoming aware of the harmony, enjoying it, smiling, and asking for more, because it feels so good. See him coming closer to you, and saying that he is now ready to mend the relationship. See the person extending a hand in friendship, or holding their arms out to embrace you, whichever would be most appropriate. Get the good feelings of this as sharp in your mind as you can, then cut off the energy flow at that point, and drop it from your mind. Forget it. Let go of it. Repeat the technique once or twice a day, until you see the results.

Here is my analysis of the technique: There are no one-sided arguments. One might say that an argument is an agreement to disagree. Both persons are at fault, and each must give in some to meet on a common ground. The one who creates the Harmony Room is taking the first step in reconciliation on a spiritual level. Since he is taking the first step on this high level, it is only fair that the other party take his first step on the physical level. In other words, the other person will usually come to you with peace overtures as a result of this mental action, as you have visualized. At least, that is the response I had when I had the opportunity to test the technique on a problem of my own, a short time after I had conceived the process.

First, I had used it on my immediate supervisor and his boss, to get some things going more smoothly. My next test was to improve relations with one of the men in our department who would have nothing to do with me. He would never speak to me in a social manner, but only to criticize me and tell me that I was doing something wrong. I decided to put him into my Harmony Room.

Imagine my surprise, when about a week later he stopped by my workbench and said, "You know Gerry, Bob and I were just talking about our boss, and we both agreed that if he ever had to leave, you would be the perfect man for the job."

Wow! What a change! Since then, we have become quite close, as the following will illustrate. This man has a habit of whistling a few bars from a song over and over, and over again. One day, when he was whistling a repetitive excerpt as he approached me on the way to one of the machines, I thought, "I'm getting tired of that tune, why doesn't he whistle *Colonel Bogey March*, or something like that?" Immediately after stopping at the milling machine, he started to whistle "Colonel Bogey." I told him what I had been thinking, and he got quite a kick out of the event.

The Harmony Room is quite flexible. If two of your friends are not getting along well with each other, you can try putting both in your Harmony Room at the same time. As you picture them there, see them talking to each other and finding out each other's good traits, and liking each other. I have used it on a church committee to help bring the group into agreement.

An example of how quickly this process can work occurred just recently. I was reading Tarot cards and doing counseling at a psychic fair, and had just given a young lady instructions in doing healing. She then asked me about her relationship with her boy friend, who was upstairs at the bar at that time. She had just had a tiff with him, and on impulse I said to her, "I've just told you how to use the Harmony Room. Let's use it now, together, on him. Create it in your mind, as

I channel healing energy to you, and then put him in the room, with the idea of bringing him into harmony, raising him above the need to have this difference with you." Then I told her that when she went up to see him, she should check to see if his attitudes had changed, then to come down to the lower level, and let me know. A few minutes later she came down the stairs, her face all smiles, and said excitedly, "He's changed! He's changed!"

The Harmony Room can also be used in conjunction with the Subconscious Examination System, to get a person to see his or her undesirable traits and to consider the possibility of change. Refer to *Section 14* for more on this technique. Use the mirror idea in the Harmony Room.

As with the other visualization techniques that I use, it is important to use the healing or creative energy along with the mental pictures. This information is given in *Chapters One and Two.* Learn to tune in on this Creative Force, and flood your Harmony Room with it, with the intention that it BE harmony. But don't stop there.

The wise person will also fill every room in his house or apartment with the same harmonious vibrations, and will also build an aura of harmony around himself that will always be with him, wherever he goes. This is not difficult to do, once you learn to receive the healing energy and start to use it. It follows the mental instructions you give to it.

Make sure that you always build up your visualizations to the highest concept that you can, and then release them at this high point. Wipe your hands together to signify the end of the process, as you are told to do when you finish sending healing to someone. Dismiss the subject from your conscious mind, so that your inner mind will attend to it.

If you find that the Harmony Room technique does not work for you, even after persistently applying yourself to it, I suggest that you examine yourself closely, to see if you are truly willing to take that first step toward the other party. Are you requiring the other party to make all the concessions? Are you willing to forgive him or her for past attitudes or actions? After carefully considering these things, try again. Set aside your negative feelings in order to use the technique, and you may create the proper atmosphere for the healing of the relationship.

SECTION 17.
Emotions as Creative Energy
-A Personal Healing-

Earlier, I stated that the best form of the creative force for healing is pure love. This is true, but *any* of the emotions can serve as the creative power, if the proper handling is used. Fear often creates negative events, of course. Other negative emotions can create changes as well, depending upon how they are used. Here is an example, from my own experience, where anger (of all things!) was the predominant force in creating a healing.

One day, in the Fall of 1942, I noticed a lump on my left wrist while I was attending a radio school in Milwaukee. The next time I went home, our family doctor removed a ganglionic cyst. In 1945, while I was in China, another cyst developed in the same location. I was using autosuggestion to help prevent further growth, with a small degree of success. After I came home, however, it continued to grow slowly. Up to this time there had been no pain, but then it started.

When the pain began, I would wrap a flexible bandage around the wrist for one day, and the pain would stop. Perhaps a month or so later, the same thing would happen, and again the bandage application would relieve it. This was repeated several times. But the time came when the pain did not stop after the application of the bandage.

At this point, I became angry with myself, and I said to myself something like this: "Damn it! I don't have to put up with this! I want this taken care of properly!" I visualized moving my wrist perfectly in any direction, and without any lump. Then I forgot about it. I do not remember how long it was until I next looked at it. It may have been the next day, or several days later, but the next time I thought to look at the wrist, the lump was gone! It has never returned, and that healing occurred over 30 years ago.

I believe that the key to this healing is in the combination of factors: a strong burst of energy (the anger), a perfect visualization, and a releasing of the whole thing from my consciousness.

CHAPTER FOUR
Mental Detection and Correction of Problems

CHAPTER FOUR
Mental Detection and Correction of Problems

SECTION 1.
Detecting and Correcting Energy Imbalance

After you have become aware of the energy and worked with it for some time, you should be able to feel another person's energy output when he is channeling it to you. Pass your hand near his hands as he directs the energy from his fingers, and you will probably feel the flow from him to you. When you can do this, you are probably ready to sense the location of areas of stress in a body.

Try the following, when you are around a person who has an injury, or some illness which involves a specific part of the body. Put a hand near the afflicted area without touching the person, and put your attention on your fingers to note any change of feeling as you do so. Look for an energy *difference,* or *a change of flow,* or a *difference in feeling* or *temperature.* As you pass your hand over the area of the injury, compare the feeling to other areas where there is no injury. I used to feel the difference as a warmth, but this changed later to a tingle, in order to avoid confusion with actual temperature differences.

These fluctuations in the aura are perceived differently by different individuals, but I find that almost anyone can perceive them once they are told how to go about it. It is not difficult to do, when you follow the procedures given here. This energy difference at an injury site might be considered as a *leak* of energy. The person is losing his life energy at that location, and the escaping energy can be felt, or even seen. Or, it is an irregularity in the aura caused by the imbalance of an injury, and the difference you feel may be the injury drawing healing energy from your hand. Regardless of the actual mechanism of the difference, there it is, and you can detect it easily.

I have emphasized, from time to time, that the healing energy is unlimited by space and time, and the same is true of the aura. You can check this easily, once you have located the "feeling" of an injury. Just picture the injured person beside you, instead of where his body really is (for instance, if he is across the room or anywhere else), and pass your hand near where you are imagining his injury to be. You will feel that same difference when your hand passes that same spot in your mind's eye. Or, if you wish, you may work it the other way around. First picture the person before you, and pass your hand near where you are imagining the injured part of his body to be, and locate the exact spot where you feel the injury to be. Then check by feeling the aura of the actual body, and you will find that you have really located it without the body being there.

I have taught this to a great many people who have never had any previous training in this field, and they were, in almost every case, able to do it the first time they tried it. When I taught a cousin to find the place in my spine where I had had some trouble, his hand was drawn directly to the spot and he could not remove his hand for a couple of minutes. This led me to believe that he had probably been a healer in a past life.

One day, when I was at home, I thought of a friend in town who has multiple sclerosis. I decided to check up on him. In my mind, I brought him to me and ran my right hand up and down his spine, and detected some difficulties in the lower third part. I started to do some healing on it, and continued for a few minutes, then rechecked his condition as I had done before. This time the aura felt much better, so I decided to call him up and check on my accuracy. He asked me how I knew he was having trouble, and I told him I had just decided to take a look. I said, "I had just finished working on it. How is it now?" and he said that it now felt all right. You see, this type of occurence can not be considered the result of suggestion. It is quite likely that many of you will be able to do the same thing: that is, detect a problem in someone else at a distance, do healing on it, then find out that the results of your healing were effective when you check with the person. When this happens, it gives a great boost to your confidence.

Some time after I had developed this diagnostic ability, it occurred to me that it should be possible to check on the past or future condition of an injury while passing the hand over the area, using the mind to attune to the time. Shortly after this, I visited an old friend of mine who had an old leg injury. I wished to check on his current condition, so I said, "Don't tell me how your leg is. I want to see if I can tell you." As I passed my hand over the area, I could feel the tingle. "Your leg is bothering you quite a bit now. Let me see if I can tell you how it was a year ago." As I passed my hand over it again, I concentrated on the idea of his condition one year before, and I felt very little of the tingle. I said, "Your leg was much better one year ago." He said, "You are absolutely right!"

I have not done extensive experimentation on this approach, but I am sure that some of you will experiment with this idea, and put it to good use. You may be able to use the same technique to tell just when an injury or illness is going to be healed, by attuning the mind to the future instead of to the past.

Since space and time are conscious agreements about reality, we need not be limited by how far away the sick person is from us. Although the aura is usually considered to extend only a few inches from the body, it can act as though it extends to infinity!

Trouble Shooting

There are other methods of locating the trouble spots. You may be able to feel in your own body exactly where the ill person is having trouble, just by *being* the person for a moment. In general, however, it is best to stay away from this method unless you know how to *be* yourself again quickly, to avoid taking on the sick person's troubles. I know this sounds silly to many people who are not familiar with the field, but there are many people who have taken on their parent's illnesses because they have been told, "You are just like your father," (or mother, or someone else) so many times. They have identified with that parent to such an extent that they take on the same illness as the parent.

You may be able to *see* trouble spots in the patient, by deliberately blurring your vision as you look at him, while imagining that your vision is penetrating his body. This tends to partly shut down physical sight, and allow the pineal *third eye* or inner sight to take effect. This will work well for some people.

Some psychics just tune in and *know* what is wrong with a person. If you do not know, there is nothing wrong in asking the patient what is wrong with him. Some healers prefer not to know, so they can more easily visualize perfection. You do not have to know what is wrong with a person in order to be of help to him. As you develop into a better channel and increase in spirituality, however, you should also develop your intuition to the point where you know the information without even trying for it.

There are some devices that are used for diagnosis of the physical body. These devices really have no diagnostic abilities of their own, but serve only as crutches or readouts for the natural ability of the operator's mind. *All the data is already in the mind.*

Such a device is used by many chiropractors to indicate which vertebrae are out of position, and to indicate when the proper correction is achieved. The *indicator* is a flat plate which is stroked by the fingers of one hand, as the *sensor* part is held next to the spine. As the sensor is passed over a misaligned vertebra, the friction between the plate and the fingers increases, so the operator knows which vertebra is causing the trouble. How does this change in friction occur? Remember that the healing force is capable of affecting anything in the Universe, and remember that all knowledge is already within each of us. It is, therefore, not difficult for this force to change the coefficient of friction between the fingers and the plate.

It is my opinion that the circuitry contained in this diagnostic device does nothing measurable in its function. An electrical current, flowing in the coil of the sensor plate, would in *no* way be able to change the plate-to-finger friction, anyway. It is the creative force within, manifesting the knowledge which is already in the mind.

Dowsing Rods and Pendulums
Muscle Testing

Dowsing rods and pendulums are also used for diagnostic purposes, since both are indicators used to change inner knowledge into physical movement.

Another system I have seen demonstrated is *muscle testing*. In this system, the patient is told to hold an arm out straight to the side, shoulder level and the person doing the testing tries the strength of the arm by pushing down on it while the patient tries to resist. By questioning or by touching various parts of the body are focused on, and the arm's resistance to the pressure is checked. When a defective or malfunctioning part of the body is mentioned or touched, the arm's resistance is lowered by the subconscious mind, and the arm therefore goes down more easily.

Handled properly, this can be an effective means of diagnosis. Full information on every disease, as well as the general health of any person, is always there in that person's subconscious mind. One drawback of muscle testing, however, is that its' accuracy can be affected by the beliefs, expectations and limitations of the *operator*, since the operator is *part* of the sensing system. That is, the beliefs, expectations and limitations of the operator can increase or decrease his arm strength as he pushes down on the arm of the patient, and thus change things enough to falsify the interpretation of the test results.

Of course, one should not neglect standard medical diagnosis any more than the standard medical community should ignore the possibilities of spiritual healing, or any other alternative system of treatment.

It is true that some people who serve as healing channels do not want to know what is wrong with the patient when they pray for his healing. It seems to me, however, that as a person becomes a better and better channel and grows spiritually, he will more accurately know what is in need of correction, will be able to sense when it is corrected, and may even know what caused the condition in the first place. After all, God already knows this data, and it is also contained in the inner mind of the patient. It is also present in my inner mind, and yours. The problem lies in getting it through the obstacles in the conscious mind, to our conscious awareness. As we grow spiritually and get rid of more of these obstacles, this inner information flows more freely, and thus becomes more accurate.

As your healing ability increases, your ability to detect and correct energy imbalance will probably increase as well, if you apply yourself to it. Some healers feel the patient's imbalance in their own bodies. Others detect it by feeling or seeing it in the aura of the patient. I am sure that there are many other ways in which it can be done, but here is the way my own ability has developed; you can probably develop yours in the same, or a similar, manner if you wish.

Symbolism

I used to close my eyes to consider a person's energy balance. (I now do it with my eyes open.) If an imbalance were present, I would see in my mind's eye a slanting line, usually indicating that one side of the body had more energy than the other. Then, as I channeled energy for balance, the slanting line would start to rectify itself, and would stabilize either horizontally or vertically, signifying that balance was achieved.

After I had been using this method for a while, it started to change. The symbol for balance changed to a Latin cross. If the person were in balance with a moderate energy supply, the cross appeared straight, of a moderate size, and the cross arm was perpendicular to the upright. If an imbalance were present, the cross would be cocked to one side, or the arm would be at an angle to the upright bar. If the person were low on energy, the cross would appear smaller.

Other modifications would sometimes appear, to give me a special message about the person. For example, in considering a young lady who seemed very confused, I got the impression of two smaller crosses being attached to the horizontal arm of the cross. I interpreted this as indicating that there were two intruding entities attached to her aura. In other words, she was possessed, to a degree. A friend of mine picked up the same information, so we exorcised her. We took her back to the times when the attachments were formed, then we turned the misguided intruders over to our spirit guides for proper education and guidance.

A halo above the cross has indicated the presence of spirit guides. After channeling energy for better guidance, the symbol changed to a ring or halo in the center of the cross, showing better integration with the guides.

A ring around the entire cross has indicated a strong aura at times. At other times, it has indicated a protective shield around the person.

At a healing service I attended, some of the healers were working on a small child. As I considered her and looked at her, I saw a diagonal line intersecting the center of the cross, representing her energy field. I said to the healer sitting next to me, "She seems to have a split in her personality." He replied that she also had considerable brain damage, which was probably the cause of the split I had perceived.

Many other symbols are capable of being used to convey information about any person you are considering. You will probably have to adopt and develop your own symbols to function at your best, but some of those I mention may be useful to you.

SECTION 2.
Checking The Chakras

The next step, after detecting an imbalance, is to check on where the imbalance is located. I decided that I should be able to check each chakra or psychic center, in turn, for balance, and it occurred to me to use a plus sign (+) as an indicator of the chakra's condition. This has worked very well.

If a chakra is low on energy, the plus sign is small. If there is a lateral imbalance, and thus unequal energy to both sides of the body, the plus sign may be rotated to the right or to the left. If the chakra is open too wide as compared with the other chakras, the plus is larger than "normal." In each case of imbalance, channel energy with the thought of correcting the situation, until the symbol's appearance is changed to indicate a balance, or at least a better balance than before.

Usually the subject can feel the difference when the balance is achieved. The state of energy balance can often be achieved in a very short time. It is also possible to shift back to the unbalanced state in the twinkling of an eye, then rebalance just as quickly, to demonstrate to the person the difference in feeling caused by energy distribution.

Sometimes there is a blockage of the pathway between chakras. This appears to me as a horizontal bar or line at that location. This can usually be corrected by flowing energy back and forth between the chakras; above and below the area, and through the clogged area, until the symbol of blockage disappears and indicates a clear channel.

As your energy sensitivity develops, you will probably be able to sense where each chakra is. You might look in some of the books on Yoga for charts showing where the major centers are located, but a more accurate and useful method is to locate the chakras in your own being.

Let us start with the **crown chakra**, above the head. Hold your right hand about one or two inches above your head, and visualize creating an energy spin, about six inches in diameter, between your hand and your head. Make it rotate clockwise, as viewed from below, or counterclockwise, as viewed from above. Then, move your hand up and down an inch or so, and note what you feel as your attention is focused on that area above your head. This will tune you in to the main chakra spin, and as a result, you may become aware of a slight dizziness. That is the spin of the chakra itself.

Having done this, you may be ready to sense some (probably most) of the other major chakras in, or near, the body. Project a spin from your hand into the body *counterclockwise as viewed from in front of your body*, near the area where the chakra is supposed to be, and move the spin in and out, and back and forth until you feel a response within, which tells you that you have found it. Once you have found it, you will be able to direct other people to do the same thing. Let us check the following, in descending order, going down the body.

The **ajna center** or "third eye" is slightly above eye level, about an inch back, inside the forehead. Project an energy spin into this space in your own head from one of your fingers, *clockwise as viewed by yourself,* as your finger is pointing between your eyes. Then, move the spin around the area a little until you feel a response, which will be where the chakra is located.

Find the other chakras listed in the same manner.

The next one, seldom shown on most chakra charts, is at the **base of the skull** where it attaches to the spine, in back of the neck.

The **throat chakra** is in the area of the thyroid gland, in the lower portion of the front of the neck.

The **heart chakra** is in the area of the sternum, or breast bone.

The **solar plexus** is next, a little above the navel.

There is one in the **area of the genitals.**

One at the **base of the spine,** near the tailbone.

One **between the ankles,** as you stand or sit. As you become aware of the healing energy, you can easily feel it there by passing your hand through that area. This one is important in the health of your feet and legs.

There are many others, but these are the most important that we are concerned with in doing healing.

Now, let us consider some other aspects of energy-balancing.

SECTION 3.
Some Acupuncture Pointers
- Hypodermics and Injuries -

If our study of healing energy and its various uses is valid, we should find it easier to understand acupuncture, and its' relative, acupressure, and see the reasons for the variations in their effectiveness.

If it is true that the healing energy is where it is imagined or visualized to be, then we can understand that the visualization of the acupuncturist, as he inserts the needles, could be an important factor in the effectiveness of the treatment by any particular operator. Differences in patient response would probably be due to the belief system of the patient, and the degree of his control over his bodily energy. The acupuncturist's expectations of energy balance would tend to be fulfilled, unless countered and nullified by negative attitudes of the patient.

Acupressure is done without needles, by applying pressure (usually with the fingers) to the proper points for energy balance. Bear in mind, however, that the energy is not limited by space, and can therefore go to the correct spots for balance without being applied to any specific areas. It is not the pressure being applied that causes the energy to be balanced. *Thought itself* is the controlling force for this energy. It is the expectation of balance, coupled with the proper flow of the creative energy, that does the job. The minds of both the operator and the patient can affect the result. *The mind furnishes the control... Energy follows thought.*

You should find, therefore, that you can balance energy flows in a body, or in a part of a body, by just flowing the healing energy there, and visualizing the system in a balanced state. This can be done either by contact or at a distance. The exact method you use is not important. Perhaps you can sense the flows themselves, and any imbalance that is present. If so, fine. Just flow energy with the thought that it will go where needed, opening blocks, leveling out into a balanced flow. Then see if you can sense the results of your efforts, and make further corrections as necessary.

If you cannot yet sense the flows, you can still balance them. Your intention is important, so just flow the energy as described, until you can easily visualize them as balanced. One approach would be to use the idea of scales being out of balance, with one side heavy and the other side light. See them ending up in perfect balance as you complete your energy flows. Use any convenient analogy to serve as an indicator of the state of balance.

The daughter of a friend had an operation. Before the operation, she was given an injection in her left hip, and her whole leg was in pain because of it. Her mother called me and explained what had happened, and asked for help. My first thought was that we should visualize withdrawing the needle, undoing the damage done by the needle. My second thought, which I believe to be the more important, was that, since most doctors and nurses know little or nothing about acupuncture, it would be very easy for a hypodermic needle insertion to throw an arm or leg (or other part of the body, for that matter) out of balance. We then rebalanced the leg, and the pain left quickly.

There must be many occasions like this, where damage is done to a patient by hypodermic injections, especially when they are done while dwelling on negative thoughts, instead of the welfare of the patient. Whenever possible, the injection should be done with love and concern, and with the visualization of a quick and complete recovery.

Needles, hypodermic or otherwise, are not the only instruments capable of throwing the body off balance. Impact by any object could do the same thing. Therefore, it would be well to conclude every healing session with a visualization of all the energy flows of the patient being in proper balance.

Needle-less to say, we should all balance our own energy flows on a daily basis, to attain a higher level of well-being.

Here is an example of how you may be able to help a person using a simple balancing process. There are many people who have a chronic problem with the legs and feet. Very often, the problem lies in the imbalance of the chakra or energy center which is located between the ankles, as the person sits or stands with the feet about six or eight inches apart. If you can feel energy, just pass your hand through this area between your feet and you will feel the chakra. This chakra is seldom shown on charts depicting the major chakras, but it is important.

Balancing this chakra is a simple process. Put your left hand above your head into the area of the crown chakra, and your right hand in the space between your ankles, with the thought of balancing the foot chakra. Or, do it to the person who is having the foot and/or leg problem, if you suspect there is an imbalance. If the imbalance is there, the person will usually feel a tingle start to travel through the legs, as the energy flow increases. Try it! You do not have to touch the person to do it. Then, note if there is an improvement in the condition. Teach the person to balance his or her own chakra (with the counterclockwise energy movements), in case it should get out of balance again.

SECTION 4.
How to Use Sympathetic Acupuncture on Yourself or Others

How would you like to try some acupuncture on yourself? Here is a safe way to do it. I call it *Sympathetic Acupuncture*, as it uses the principles of sympathetic magic.

Sympathetic magic uses the principle of representing the body of the person being "worked on" with a doll or a picture, with the idea that whatever is done to the doll or picture will be experienced by the person it represents. For this treatment we could use a chart of the body showing the locations of the acupuncture points and meridians. Lacking this, you might use a regular chart of the body showing the internal organs. Decide that, for the duration of the treatment, the chart shall represent your body and its energy flows. Decide where, in your body, the energy is needed for balance. Remember that this knowledge is always present within you. Then, place needles lovingly in the chart at the places you feel need balancing, as if you were doing it in your real body, without pain. As you insert the needle, picture in your mind the energy being balanced. Observe any changes you feel occurring in your body as you do this. Use your judgment as to how long you should continue this treatment. When you are finished, remove the needles from the chart, and then be sure to *dis-identify* your body from the chart.

You could attach a label bearing your name to the chart, with the thought that the label creates your identification with the chart, and completely removes it when the label is removed. The same chart should not be used to work on another person without first *clearing it* of the previous person's identity.

"Wait a minute!," someone is sure to say, "That sounds like Voodoo!" That is right. Exactly the same principles are being used, except that in this case you are trying to heal yourself or another. If you feel that this is an evil practice and your religion forbids it, look at the results and the intention to help. Even if your "religion" seems to prohibit it, the prohibition is, most likely, a misinterpretation by some secondary follower, long removed from the founder of that religion. Certainly God permits such a thing to be done, as it follows His natural laws, working throughout the Universe. We can all use the same natural laws, regardless of our other differences.

Map dowsing is done in the same manner, by making an agreement that the pendulum or rods of the dowser will react to the location of water, metal, or other desired material, in the same way as if the dowser were there in the flesh. And it works. How does dowsing work? It is not because of radiations given off by the buried water, oil, metal pipes, or other things sought underground, because then map dowsing would never work. The real reason it works is that all knowledge is within us all. In this case, it is the knowledge of where things are in our Universe! We use the divining rod (or fork, or pendulum) to get that inner data out to the conscious mind, usually through subconscious movements of the arm or hand muscles. Many utility companies use dowsing rods in their everyday work.

In a similar manner, insect pests in a plot of land have been controlled by treating a map of the plot with insect poison, instead of applying the poison to the plot itself. It also works. See, *Magic: The Science of the Future*, by Joseph Goodavage (Signet No. 451-W7801-150, 1976). In considering the effects mentioned in Goodavage's book concerning the Hieronymous machine, bear in mind that the power is in the mind of the user, and his ability to visualize, and not in the machine at all.

Proxy healing can work in the same way. The person who is sitting in the "healing chair" for the patient (who may be far away), becomes the patient to the best of his ability, receives healing as the patient, then becomes himself again. This also works.

SECTION 5.
Diagnosis Using Charts and Pictures

If we are able to balance energy by using a chart to represent the patient's body, it should follow that we can also use that chart to find out where in the body the person is in need of healing. One way this can be done is to feel the energy changes with your hand, as you pass your hand over the chart or picture of the person; another way is to use a pendulum. Ask your inner self which pendulum movement should be used to indicate a malfunctioning organ or area of the body, while you are holding the pendulum's string or chain with one hand and gazing at the pendulum weight, not at your hand. The material of which the pendulum is made makes no difference in its operation; you can use an ordinary metal nut from a screw or bolt, tied to a piece of string or thread if you wish. It is your mind that does the work; the knowledge is within.

CHAPTER FIVE
Other Pathways
to Healing

CHAPTER FIVE
Other Pathways to Healing

SECTION 1.
Augmenting Standard Methods
of Treatment

I think it is about time that we considered the need for many other methods to achieve healing. Do not make the mistake of ignoring alternative approaches, such as medicine, manipulation (such as osteopathy, chiropractic, naprapathy, massage, etc.), and surgery. All of these, plus many others, are part of God's way of bringing us healing, and each has its' proper place.

Sometimes we may have to undergo surgery when we would rather have the problem taken care of by a miracle. Perhaps it is because we need that particular experience at that time for our own growth. It is certain that not everybody is ready to get rid of the conditions that he has created in the twinkling of an eye. But regardless of the type of treatment we are receiving, we can still benefit by using the same principles of spiritual healing and energy flow with visualization to increase the healing.

As I write this, I had to stop for a moment to fulfill a request for help from a friend who called me this morning. This illustrates the matter at hand. A friend of hers was to undergo surgery for a double bypass this morning, and she asked me for help. As I noted the time for the operation approaching, I stopped my writing and sent her friend healing energy. I saw her flooded with it, until she seemed glowing and at peace. Then, I visualized the energy being in the whole hospital area, permeating everyone, and coordinating the doctors and nurses involved with the patient, to lead to perfection in their work on her. I visualized her healing quickly and perfectly, being active and happy, and I saw my friend being thankful for the good results, as well. Since the visualization was rather easy to achieve, I knew that the results would be good.

Seven Steps to Healing

Here are a few things you can do to help, in whatever system of treatment is to be used, either for yourself or another.

1. Mentally "plug in" the doctor, therapist, or nurses to a healing group, or the healing power, or to the

Christ Consciousness, however you conceive of it. If you don't know of a healing group, you can decide to plug in to our healing class, which has met on Thursday mornings for years.

A friend of mine, who had an injured back as the result of an accident, was going to a naprapath for treatment. He had attended our class a few times. "It was odd," he said to me. "I was expecting to feel the same healing energy from the naprapath's hands that I had felt coming from the healing class. I was disappointed." I said to him, "You have another appointment tonight. Why don't you visualize his hands being *plugged in* to the healing class's energy field, and note the difference? It should work." It did! He could feel the difference, and so could the doctor.

2. Visualize cooperation among all persons working on or for the patient.

3. Visualize the beneficial action of any drugs being used as having greater effect, so that lower dosages are needed.

4. IMPORTANT! Visualize the negative side-effects of drugs or radiation treatment as being eliminated or reduced, with the elements that cause negative side-effects draining harmlessly out of the patient's system.

5. Visualize a rapport between doctors, nurses, and patient that will lead to better diagnosis and correction of the prime cause of the disorder.

6. Visualize a perfect balance of the mind-and-body forces, to aid in faster and better healing, following any system of treatment.

7. Visualize the family and friends of the patient being thankful that the patient is healed, happy, and free of the problem.

A standard cry of the medical establishment, concerning spiritual healing or other alternate methods of treatment, is that the patient who visits the "quack" may be building up false hopes and thus be prevented from getting the proper treatment. There are no guarantees, however, that the patient is going to get a doctor who is competent to resolve his problem. A medical degree conferred on a person is no certification of competence in healing. Even if a doctor is competent, we can not be sure that his method of treatment will bring healing to you as an individual.

The possibility exists that that your personality requires an unorthodox method of treatment to successfully treat your illness and bring healing. If such unorthodox methods are prohibited by law, then those laws are, in effect, denying your healing. If it can be shown that physical touch is not a necessary factor in spiritual healing (and it can), then any laws against laying-on-of-hands are ridiculous and meaningless, and should be repealed.

I would like to point out that I am not against doctors. Many doctors are good, and some of them are using the principles of spiritual healing in their everyday practice, but they dare not call attention to the fact. All methods of healing are needed on this earth. We do not all respond to medicine, nor to herbal remedies, nor to acupuncture, nor to any other single system, including "faith" healing. For proper healing, we must have faith in the method used. Every method is needed by somebody.

With the increased interest and research into *psychic* or *spiritual* healing, some people are saying, "We need an organization to accredit the healers, to decide which ones should be allowed to practice." Now, that sounds pretty good, at first thought. But the real question is this: Who is going to have the foresight to see what miracles are going to be wrought through each healer? We don't very often produce healings on demand, do we? The patient must always be ready for such a healing to occur.

Sometimes a beginning healer, even a child, is the channel for an instantaneous healing, without any training. There is no way you can logically evaluate the healing potential of any individual. Then, too, who is going to decide which healers should be allowed to practice? Certainly not a medical organization. They are not experts in the field. An organization to accredit healers is just as ridiculous as prohibiting the laying-on-of-hands, unless the organization consists of psychics and healers able to discern the healing potential of each applicant.

An alternative course would be to make the information on healing available to so many people of all walks of life, including open-minded doctors, that the benefits of these procedures would be self-evident. We must get rid of the false idea that only a special group can be healers. If each of us teaches several others even a little bit about this great healing force and how to use it, the total effect upon the welfare of the people will be tremendous. More people will start to become aware that they are creating the circumstances of their own lives, and consequently, will do something about creating better futures for themselves and their families. Our thoughts, when properly handled, will serve as preventive therapy to increase our health. Healing groups will unite their creative efforts, to heal problems other than sickness, with great success.

One step in the right direction, of course, is the teaching of *Therapeutic Touch* to nurses. As we have seen, in most cases, an actual physical touch is not necessary to be effective. The information contained in this book could be of great value to both doctors and nurses in achieving a higher percentage of healings, if these techniques are practiced.

SECTION 2.
Negating the Effects of Alcohol

In *item 4* of the previous section, I mentioned negating the effects of some drugs with healing techniques. A number of the readers of this material will have difficulty in believing that the negative or side-effects of drugs can be negated by these methods of spiritual healing. The following technique and its' success might be one means of convincing some of you doubters that it can be done.

It is relatively easy to sober up a person who has been drinking, and thus "has a buzz on." I have done it on several occasions, and the effect usually takes place very quickly. Hold your hands over the person's head and visualize the white light coming down through the person and negating the effects of the alcohol on the person's consciousness, thus restoring the mind to a sober condition. It usually takes less than a minute to achieve a significant difference, if the person agrees to the process. Try it on someone; you will find that it works. It can also be done with hypnosis, but this method is simpler and quicker.

Hypnosis uses the same creative energy as the healer uses, to give reality to the hypnotic suggestions, regardless of whether the hypnotist knows anything about the energy or not. By the way, Mesmer's "animal magnetism" is the same force.

How is this *sobering healing* possible? Consider this: Any effect that drugs can create in the mind, can also be done with the mind alone. The mind is a non-physical thing. It is very easy to create the effect of drinking alcohol in a hypnotic subject, so he feels the same as if he had really been drinking something alcoholic instead of just water. The result is an altered state of consciousness, that of drunkenness. This sobering healing is merely doing the same thing in reverse. My thoughts and intentions, plus the creative energy, change the consciousness back to normal.

CHAPTER SIX
Further Tips and Miscellany

CHAPTER SIX
Further Tips and Miscellany

It would be well to point out the benefits to be derived from concentrating on healing specific parts of the body in some cases, rather than just visualizing a "whole" person, and letting it go at that.

Illness, in various parts of the body, can be caused by a multitude of things. I would refer you to Alice Steadman's book, *Who's the Matter with Me?* It is a very enlightening book. A person may be ready for healing in one part of the body, but not ready to part with the cause of the problem in another part, so your visualization of perfection of the whole person might not take effect. In such a case, it would probably be better to concentrate your healing abilities on each organ or part of the body, in turn. By this approach, each visualization which is ready to be manifested as healing may be more easily attained.

A good practice for all of us to follow is to thank each part of our bodies, every day, for its contributions and cooperation, and for the improvements to follow. This is an old yoga principle, which will help to unite the body/mind forces. You can imagine the effects of always saying or thinking, "That darn arm of mine!," or "This stomach of mine always gives me trouble!" You seldom realize that the facts are quite the opposite, and that it is you who are creating the trouble for the stomach. Hopefully, the technique of thanking each body part will help to break the habit of condemning one's body, which is only following orders given to it by the mind.

Working on a person desiring healing, I pray for guidance in the application of the proper techniques, including inspirations to try new approaches as they are needed. Sometimes the prayer should be for "best possible results," instead of for a specific healing. This is especially important when you have a difficult time visualizing the patient being healed. Use your intuition.

It would be well to practice spinning and vibrating the energy. I used to think that this was all imagination and meant nothing. Then I found that others could quite easily sense what I was doing. It was real. Sometimes I run an energy spin back and forth through the area of congestion or tension, with the intention in mind to break the pattern of the problem. After I do this, I visualize the area functioning perfectly. *Be sure to give the spin or vibration a direction or purpose!*

As might be imagined, if you have an outstandingly good characteristic in your own health pattern, you will probably have more than usual success in bringing healing to others with that problem. For example, my digestion is seldom bothered by anything I eat. I can eat almost anything, as far as foods are concerned. If I should catch the flu, which is quite rare, I recover very quickly. I believe that explains what happened in the following case.

I called up a friend whom I had not seen for some time. When I asked how she was, she said that she had the flu. I told her that I would channel healing to her, and started to do so immediately. I continued talking, as this does not interfere with the healing, and may add to the rapport as well. After a few minutes, she said, "Gerry, my fever's gone!" A week later, when I again talked to her, she said that the flu stopped at the same time, as far as she could tell.

I have found that the *Calming and Relaxing Method* described previously, is very effective in treating the flu, and other digestive disturbances. Aim the healing toward the stomach and the intestines. In your mind, see the whole system calming down, everything functioning in a healthy manner. Visualize the various bodily flows perfectly balanced to achieve the healing.

If you listen carefully when an illness is described to you, you may get a clue as to the best way to cope with the problem. For example, a woman came to me for a Tarot reading at a psychic fair, and said, "I've had a buzzing in my left ear for a long time, and nobody has been able to help me." I said, "I'll see what I can do," and I went to stand behind her. "It sounds like a waterfall," she continued. For some reason, that phrase seemed important in my mind. I put a hand near each ear; with my left hand I started to use the *pulling technique*, and visualized pulling the water from the waterfall, until in my mind, the waterfall had decreased to a mere trickle. I said, "Has it changed any?" "Yes, it has changed to a ringing," she answered. I then put my hands on both ears and continued to flow energy, and said, "Tell me when it's gone." In a moment, it was indeed gone. She told me that the buzz changed to a ringing, which faded away in the distance as I continued to flow energy, until it was entirely gone.

Under usual conditions, I have no difficulty in illustrating and demonstrating energy flows. While working on this section of the book, however, my wife and I visited friends in Wisconsin. My health, at that time, was not up to its usual level, although I was not aware at that moment of just how low my energy level was. When I tried to direct some energy to the fingertips of my friends, I was surprised to find that they could not feel it, and neither could I! Having an intestinal disturbance at the time, I spent some time in energy-gathering exercises, and visualization of a properly-functioning digestive system. The next day I was fine, and was able to demonstrate energy flows to a cousin with no difficulty.

I wish to make a specific point here, with reference to the above. Notice that, while I was depleted, I could not demonstrate the energy flows so that it could be felt. That was evidently because I needed the energy I was taking in, so I could not at that moment pass it on to another *just for a demonstration*. I am certain, however, that in the future, *if the other person is in need of healing*, I can if necessary, use an alternate method of channeling energy to him, whether I am depleted or not. For instance, just visualize the person being surrounded and filled with healing energy, and it is there without it having to run through your own body. *There is no shortage of energy: there is plenty for all.*

SECTION 1.
The Importance of Intention

Nothing happens to us during our lifetimes without there being a cause leading up to it. It is usually fairly easy to push pain out, but this is not our only goal as healers. We intend to do what we can to correct the cause of the illness. The correction must be done by overriding or canceling the original intention (to be sick or disabled), that the person has installed in his mind, for sometimes over a period of many years.

I know that many persons will say, "But I never intended to be sick! It was an accident, and just happened!" This is generally true, as far as the conscious levels of the mind are concerned. But how often have you thought that it would be nice to have some free time, then found yourself sick, with lots of free time, only you were too sick to enjoy it? This is an example of an incomplete prayer being answered in an undesirable way, because your mental pictures were not completed properly. Keep in mind, that a prayer does not have to be verbalized; your emotions of either desire or repulsion supply the necessary creative energy. A good psychic might pick up the coming sickness or accident before it occurrd, sometimes a long time in advance.

You might pick up the data in your dreams, if you learn to interpret your symbols properly, and thus you may be able to circumvent many unpleasant events, by heeding the warnings that your inner self tries to get through to you.

We read now of some doctors studying the palms of babies, for signs indicating a predisposition to develop certain types of heart disease. This shows that the pattern for the illness is already in existence, and will be materialized sometime in the future, unless certain factors (possibly involving decisions and attitudes) are changed, thus making the illness unnecessary for the development of the individual.

Many problems that people are experiencing in the present time are continuations of unresolved or unhealed problems that they have had in a past life. The problems have been restimulated in the present by the individual being with the same people they were with in the past life. The final chapter in this book shows you how you can help to heal the problems carried over from past lives. I have been doing this for several years, with good success. Folks, *when you heal the past you also heal the present, and therefore the future!*

The future can be changed, and so can the lines in your hand, as in palmistry. Ask an expert palmist. Some of them have recorded such changes in a person's hands, as the person has made major changes in himself. I have seen such changes.

We are constantly giving ourselves problems. We are likely to solve these more readily, once we recognize the *problems* as *opportunities for growth,"* and start looking at ourselves more closely to see where we are not living up to our ideals.

Each person's body is a perfect representation of what that person's spirit has created for his development, and is the total result of his own past. I believe that if we were to make a thorough study of what are called *"spontaneous remissions"* of illness, we would find that in each case there was something that happened within the person, a change in growth which made the illness no longer necessary for the person's development. As a result, the person was healed.

The intention to be sick, or to have an accident, or to have a happy and healthy life, can lie deep within a person's being. The things that happen to us are intended for our spiritual growth. When we have fully learned the lessons we are supposed to learn, we should be ready for the healing of the difficulty. Therefore, when something negative happens to us, it would be best to thank God at once for the experience, as well as for the subsequent healing. And, ask Him that we might quickly learn the full lesson from it, so that we might more quickly receive the healing. Thus our *intention* to learn helps to lead us in the right direction. Please don't put the blame for the negative experience on anyone else. It is *YOUR* universe and *YOUR* creation.

Although the *intention to be sick*, or any other negative intention, is seldom on a conscious level, it can be rather close at times, especially when the subject is trying to control someone in his area by the act of being incapacitated, so that he has to be waited upon. Note that the wide use of headaches to control others! Sometimes the cause of experiencing an illness or injury may originate in a curious thought, such as, "I wonder what that suffering person feels like?" If your creativity goes high enough, you could find out in a hurry, and painfully.

I believe that the intention to have a problem (or opportunity for growth, depending upon how you look at it) can exist at various levels within a person, and can be carried over long periods of time, from one lifetime to another, since time is not a limiting factor as far as the creative energy is concerned.

I do not profess to know how all such intentions are contained within the individual, but I am quite certain that *each of us creates our own realities, and we have nobody else to blame for whatever happens to us.*

If you have a persistent *negative* condition, it is a good idea to make a list of all the things you have learned from having the condition that have helped you to become a better person. This may lead to a quicker or more complete healing.

Your intention to become a healing channel is the single most important factor in becoming one, as then you are always given more ability to carry out that intention, as you apply what ability you have.

As you channel energy for healing, visualize the patient's "inclination to be sick" being replaced with an "intention to be healthy, happy, and helpful to others."

It is said that the bite of a human is very dangerous. Why would that be so? It is not necessarily because there are great numbers of bacteria in the mouth. It is more likely to be because of the *intention* behind the bite.

Here is my explanation: The saliva is charged with prana, or life energy. Keep in mind that all forces can be used for either constructive or destructive purposes. The intention is what determines the result. Therefore, when one person bites another with the intention to cause hurt, it is the creative energy in the saliva that promotes the infection, and not just the fact that there are germs in the mouth. The same person could lick a wound with loving thoughts of healing it, with the same germs present, and thereby assist in healing. A dog's bite is probably dangerous for the same reason. My wife, Phyllis, tells me that years ago, their dog cared for their kittens, who had infected eyes, by holding the kittens one by one and licking their eyes, until they were healed.

From this viewpoint, note the tendency to put an injured finger to the mouth, or to "kiss a hurt, to make it better."

SECTION 2.
Taking on the Problems of Another

Words of caution are needed here. Whenever you are going to do healing for another, do not approach the project with the idea, "I'm going to *take* the illness (or disease) from this person," because you may find that you will thereby acquire the problem or its symptoms for yourself. Instead, conceive of the idea that you are serving as the channel to *give* the person *healing,* and not taking anything from him. Taking on for yourself another's illness is not necessary, or desirable, yet there are healers who do this, only because they expect it to happen, and do not know how to avoid it. Or, they do it because they think that that is the only way the person can be healed.

That idea, however, is false. In our Universe, each one creates his or her own realities, whether they seem to be blessings or curses. You cannot take for yourself another's problem. You can only buy for yourself another problem just like it. The other person may receive a healing because of your concern for him, but only if he is ready for it to happen; because he has learned his lesson and is truly through with it.

I occasionally encounter a person who has made a pact or agreement, within himself, to take another person's illness, with the provision that the ill person be healed, and this indeed occurred. I believe that such persons have great potential as healing channels, if they would understand that you don't have to take on the ill conditions for yourself, but simply act as a channel to help create the healing. If you become loaded down with the problems you have taken on from another, you will soon become too incapacitated to be a good channel to help anyone.

SECTION 3.
How to Charge an Object or Space with Energy
- Blessing a House -

You are now able to put an energy charge on an object, by flowing the energy to it, with the decision that the energy remain in the object until it is touched by someone needing the energy, or with some other purpose in mind.

It may be done in any way that you can conceive, but here are a few suggestions.

1. Hold the object in one hand. Open the other hand, and pull in energy with it, visualizing the energy filling the object and charging it fully, making it radiant. You will feel the energy flowing, so you will know it is going. To check, set the object down, and pass a hand over it to feel the charge that is there. Simple, isn't it?

2. Lay the object in an open palm, and visualize the energy being pulled or drawn into it from all directions. Check your results, as before.

3. Set the object down. Open one palm to collect energy, and aim the energy at the object with the other hand. Check to see if others can feel the charge, as well. This proves it is not your imagination.

4. Simply visualize the energy entering the object from all directions, or already being there in the object. This is probably the easiest way to do it at a distance. Charge something in another part of your house in this manner, and then check as before.

5. Pick an open doorway. Decide that you are going to put a charge in the *space* of the doorway, and proceed to do it. Then see if others can feel it, as they walk through the doorway. As you energize the area, give the energy a particular purpose or intention, to create a certain effect. Experiment in creating a tingle, or a warmth, or a coolness, or a feeling of harmony, or some other effect, then note the reaction of your friends as they walk through it. Some will feel it easily, and others will not.

Remember, that the energy follows the purpose you put behind it. Give it duration and usefulness. You can put a charge on jewelry, for instance, to surround the wearer with an awareness of God's presence; to increase the health; to keep the person in higher spirits; to pick up the person's energy level; to prevent energy losses; as a lucky charm; or any other purpose you have in mind.

6. Here is one way to bless a house. You can use a picture of the house, or a sketch of it, or just draw a rectangle or square on a piece of paper, or use a small box to represent the house. If this is not convenient to use, you can even imagine that the house is right in front of you, greatly reduced in size. Whatever you use, let it represent the house to be blessed. Imagine that you are much greater in size than the house, and put both your hands over the visualized house. Visualize a white light coming from above, through your hands and entering the house (in the same manner of healing as described in *Healing Method 4*). If you are blessing the house of another person, have him or her, or other occupants join with you. I usually say something like this:

"Let us visualize a white light coming down from God, through our hands, and filling the whole house -- lighting up the whole place -- forgiving all the past problems -- creating harmony among all who live here -- increasing communication between the occupants -- creating better health conditions -- raising the spirits of all -- getting rid of all negative influences -- protecting from violence and theft -- drawing God's blessings to all. See the whole house glowing with this holy energy, so that as people approach the area, they can sense the difference, and feel the peace. See this aura growing,

spreading the influence further from the house, so these bene-
ficial effects extend quite a distance from the house itself. See
this creation being there until you decide to change it. See all
thanking God for the blessing." Then wipe your hands of it,
and consider it to be done.

This technique usually makes an instant improvement in the way the house feels. At a psychic fair,
some time ago, a young lady and I blessed her house to
rid it of the negative vibrations caused from the difficulties between her ex-husband and herself. About a half-
hour later, she came to me again, and said, "I just had to
come back and tell you what happened. I live not far
from here. I went home, and when I stepped into the
house, it felt so different I had to burst out laughing!"
She told me much later that it stayed that way for a long
time.

If you examine some of the magazine ads, you
will see quite a number of advertisements on "magic
amulets," or "lucky crosses," or various other so-called
secret ways of getting: riches, health, a girl, a man, or
many other things. They ALL work because of the
power YOU give them. Some of them are, no doubt,
charged with energy, to help you achieve the results.
Some may have magnets to *attract* your wishes, but do
not confuse this creative energy with a magnetic field. A
magnetic field is space-and-time limited, a physical
phenomenon, and the creative energy is not. What I am
getting at is that *you can create your own personal lucky
charms, simply by charging them with energy for a purpose.*
As you develop control, you will be able to store
the energy in an object until a specific person touches it,

if you wish. That is, only the person you intend to receive the energy will be able to tap the supply. The key is in your intention, your expectation, and your visualization. A glass of water or a bottle, may be charged with energy, and then given to a sick person to drink, sometimes with very beneficial results. According to recent and current scientific research, when a healer charges water, it changes the hydrogen bonding characteristics of the water, which can be measured in the laboratory. It is *not* just imagination, suggestion, or *faith*, although we cannot work effectively without the element of faith in what we are doing. After all, the creative force does follow thought and expectation. In other words, *expect a miracle!*

SECTION 4.
The Converter Nut

One day I picked up horse chestnuts, or "buckeyes," as they are called, and put them in my pocket. I recalled that there is an old practice of carrying a buckeye to ward off rheumatism and arthritis, and realized that, for certain people, the practice was effective -- not from any element or quality in the nut, but because of their belief. Then I thought, "There is no reason why I cannot put an energy charge on one of these nuts to fulfill a specific purpose." I proceeded as follows:

I held the nut in one hand and directed energy to it, thinking that the charge should be self-sustaining, drawing from the universal supply to maintain its charge; that the charge would convert the bearer's negative emotions and forces to positive ones (since all emotions are the same energy); and to increase his general health and his awareness of God within him.

Having done this, I tested the reality of it. I handed the nut to a friend who is able to feel any emotion she wants to, and told her to put herself into apathy, which would be defined as a "way-down-at-the-bottom" emotion of hopelessness. She told me that, even as she put herself down there, she felt the crown chakra above the head moving up, to raise her to a higher level. It was working! Another friend tried it, and said she bounced right back up; it immediately lifted her spirits.

I took a supply of the charged nuts to a psychic fair where I was doing some readings, and I gave a nut to each person for whom I read. A few minutes after I finished reading for a lady, she came back over to me and said, "I felt you should know that I have had a bladder infection, but when you put that nut in my fingers, the irritation stopped immediately." Four months later she came to see me at the next psychic fair at the same place, where she introduced me to her friend as "the man who healed her." I told her it was not I who did it; it was her own energy. The irritation, the pain, the bleeding, all stopped at once. The energy charge had converted her negative or destructive force to a positive or constructive one, and thus healed her.

Since then, I have given away many of these "converter nuts," as I call them. I have also put similar charges on items of jewelry, and taught many others to do the same. You can do it, too, by following the instructions on flowing energy. It should be borne in mind that, although the energy charge will tend to fulfill the intention given it, *nothing* external can overcome the individual's own FREE WILL. He can remain as miserable and sick as his own being chooses.

Why doesn't the energy charge drain off as it does its' work? In the first place, the charge is *intended* to be self-sustaining, to replenish itself when needed. Remember, energy follows thought. Secondly, the charge is intended to serve only as a catalyst, to convert the negative vibrations to positive ones. No energy is being used to do this. The same energy is being used, and given a new set of vibrations. The catalyst remains unchanged while it does its job.

Other intentions can be put into the energy charge in the nut, or in other objects, if desired. Just hold that intention in mind as you flow the energy into it, then focus on the feeling "it is done," and release it.

Occasionally, a person will say that he can't carry the nut with him, or asks, "What if I don't have it with me when I need it?" Then I show him how space has no effect upon its working. I have him hold the nut in his hand, and feel the vibrations in it. Then I have him set the nut down, and close his hand as though he were still holding it. He will then feel the energy in his hand, as though it were still there! Be sure to try this, if you have not already done so.

Some people will not feel the energy charge at all, and will thus ridicule all this. Just about any child to whom you hand a charged object, will easily feel the charge, however, usually as a tingle (without having to be told what to look for), so it cannot be attributed to suggestion. Children are very sensitive.

SECTION 5.
How to "Tune In" on the Vibrations at Another Location

As you become more aware of this wonderful energy we have been discussing and manipulating, you will probably become more aware of the emotional flows of those around you, and also the general character of the "vibrations" around you, as you go from one place to another. If you have reached this state in your development, it is a simple step to tell what the vibrations are at any other place, in much the same manner as you can feel any person's aura at a distance.

Since we all are part of God, we too, are throughout all space and time, but our attention is usually on the body we are inhabiting. *Clairvoyance,* or "seeing clearly at a distance," also known as "remote viewing," works by putting your attention on that part of your soul which is already there, to observe what is happening at that location, wherever (and whenever) it may be. It is not necessary to project an *astral body* there to observe. Just imagine you are there at the distant location, and decide that you can feel the vibrations that exist at that location. If you have visited a location where the vibrations are extraordinary, practice being there and feeling them over again.

It does not matter whether you imagine you are

at the distant location, or imagine bringing the distant place to where *you* are; both methods work.

Once you have achieved this ability, the next step is to do the same thing with a time shift; or tune in on the vibrations associated with a past event. If you are a Christian, or even if you are not, a good example is the event of the Last Supper, with Jesus and His disciples. Put yourself there in your mind, and experience the tremendous energy field that was (and is) there! Our weekly healing class has done this as a group a number of times, usually on Maundy Thursday.

The first time we tried it, we were meeting at a friend's house. One of the members arrived late, after we had started. He told us later that, when he stepped into the house, it was like stepping into a tangible wall of energy.

You can visit other sacred places, of course, pertaining to religions other than Christianity.

Incidentally, you will achieve this attunement more easily if you do it with a group of others, due to the *group effect*. The group's total power is greater than the sum of the individual parts.

Remember the old radio program "You Are There!"? Now, with this technique, you can check ancient events for yourself. Perhaps you may come up with more accurate information than can be found in books. As I write this, the thought comes to me that you could check on the confusion and fears present when Atlantis was in the process of sinking! That one is a dandy! Don't try it, however, if you tend to panic easily.

There are plenty of happy experiences to explore, and there is no point in seeking trouble. Explore your Universe throughout time and space!

SECTION 6.
The Akashic Records

We have read and heard about the *akashic records*, which are defined as being the records of all that has happened since the "beginning," whatever that means. Some people, in either dreams, trance, or meditation, have seen these records pictured as large books, with all the information recorded within. At the present time, I realize that books are necessary only on the physical plane. As the soul exists throughout all time and space, all knowledge is recorded within each one of us, and is probably available to us through our attunement with God and our inner beings.

I believe that the preceding technique, of *tuning in on distant times and places*, is a means of starting to become aware of the akashic records. I believe that contacting these records will turn out to be much easier than people have been led to expect. After all, Edgar Cayce indicated that anyone could do what he could do, if he devoted himself to the project.

If ALL knowledge is within each person, and if we can get rid of some of the limitations we have put on our abilities and capabilities, by using these techniques we may be able to fill in some of the gaps in our history, and reveal some of the true happenings which have been considered as "secret." There are no secrets from God, who is always within all of us.

SECTION 7.
Some Thoughts About "Pyramid Power"

Much fuss has been made about the energy collected by a pyramid shape, since the publication of Ostrander and Schroeder's book, *Psychic Discoveries Behind the Iron Curtain* (Prentice-Hall, Inc., 1970). Since then, many companies have been in business supplying pyramids of all sizes, to do such things as bring healing, sharpen razor blades, change the taste of drinks, dry foods without spoiling, improve crops, increas luck; over-the-bed pyramids to improve your sleep, pyramid amulets, pyramid hats and tents for aiding meditation, and about everything else you can think of to do with them.

Buildings, including houses, have been made in the pyramid shape, as well.

The *pyramid effect* is real. The shape does seem to gather energy, the same energy with which we have been working. Why does the pyramid gather energy? Let us consider a couple of the "discoveries" about pyramids. The point of focus for the energy was supposed to be *within* the pyramid, at the place corresponding to the location of the King's Chamber, in the Great Pyramid of Gizeh. Then later, someone arranged small pyramids in groups with the bases fastened together, and we were told that the energy was now focused *above* the apex, so you could charge something with energy merely by placing it on top of the array. What is the reason for the change of function?

Let us now consider the question of orientation. Opinion is divided, with some "experts" saying it must be aligned with *true* North, and others saying that it must be aligned with the *magnetic* North. Again, these ideas are based on the accurate north-south orientation of the Great Pyramid. Some pyramids sold contain a small magnet in the base, so they will always be aligned correctly with their own magnetic field, for maximum energy collection, in any position. Again, what is the reason for these conflicting ideas working as they do?

According to my analysis, the cause of these varied effects is the expectation for the pyramid shape to gather energy. It has nothing to do with the actual shape, or the other conditions mentioned. Remember, that the energy follows the thoughts given it. If you visualize it being at a certain place, it *is* there. One of the items that led me to this conclusion is the information that some people were using *only the idea or mental image* of a pyramid over their razor blades to keep them sharp. An actual pyramid was not needed to achieve the same result.

Furthermore, you can make an outline of a pyramid that will collect energy. Pipes, with the proper connections for making pyramids large enough to sit under for meditation, or to put over your bed, are being sold. These pyramid outlines collect as much energy as the solid ones do. It is the *idea* of a pyramid collecting energy that causes the energy to collect.

Now, let us look at the magnetic orientation question, and the practice of putting a magnet in the pyramid's base, to allow it to collect energy in any position, instead of having to align it with the north-south direction. In the first place, the earth's magnetic lines of force can be considered as relatively straight, unless diverted by magnetic deposits in the earth. They are probably fairly straight at the Gizeh location. This Great Pyramid is considered the "model" for the perfect pyramid.

Consider a small pyramid with a magnet in its base, and the configuration of its resultant magnetic field. The field of a bar magnet is essentially of a toroid (doughnut) shape; the lines of force are circular, more or less, so the magnetic field penetrating and surrounding the small pyramid with its own "correcting" magnet looks *completely different* from the field near and in the Great Pyramid. Yet, the addition of that magnet, according to some, will add to that small pyramid's energy-collecting abilities. Why? Not because of any real meaning to the configuration of the magnetic field, but because of the *expectation* of the effect on energy-collection.

Energy Collection Experiment

Here is a simple experiment that you can easily do to illustrate the truth of this energy collection. Draw a circle, approximately two or three inches in diameter, on a piece of paper. Then, visualize energy being drawn to the space inside the circle. Picture the circle radiating strongly with the energy. As soon as you have a good visualization of its radiating energy, you will find that you can feel the energy difference with your hand, and so can others. It works that simply!

Pyramids are not the only designs being used to gather energy. Flat plates have been made with weird and unusual designs on them, worn on a chain around the neck. Some of these are made of metallic-clad (sometimes silver or gold) insulating material, then etched to leave only the complex metallic design. Some of these were designed by Pat Flanagan, who has been considered by some to be an "expert" in pyramid energy and related fields. These plates collect energy because that is what the design was *intended* to do, and not because there is any special "magic" in the design itself. You see, an ordinary design is too ordinary to collect much energy. You don't expect it to do much, and so it doesn't. But when you see a new, beautiful, intricate pattern of precious metal on one of these plates, it draws your attention, and the viewer thinks, "Wow! That must *really* collect energy!" Attention usually projects energy to the object observed. The *intention* to draw attention causes it to do so.

The above ideas can be proven by simple experiments, by you and your friends. Make your own energy-gathering designs, and you will discover that they do work, if you intend and expect them to do so.

The Yogic philosophy says that all is "maya," or illusion, a creation of our own beings. The Sutras of Patanjali state that, in order to perceive anything in our universe, *we* must first put it there. The Universe we perceive is, to a large extent, created *by common agreement*. If we put this universe together with our collective thoughts, there can be no special shape which is a better collector of energy, unless *we* create it that way.

While looking at the reproduction of the Great

163

Seal of the United States on the reverse of a dollar bill, I conceived of a "spoof" idea to pull on pyramid buffs. I put an energy charge on the space where the pyramid is shown. Then, I turned the bill over and considered the front side, opposite the pyramid. I held in my mind the idea of a shield being in the paper, which would not allow the energy charge to be felt from the front. The charge on the pyramid was conceived to be self-sustaining, so it will not leak off. I kept the bill separate from the others in my wallet, so I could show it at any time. However, if I should get it mixed up with the others, it can be easily distinguished from the others by its charge, or I can easily charge another one. The following is how I used it.

I would usually say, "Let me show you some REAL pyramid energy," as I got the bill out. "Feel the energy charge here, over the pyramid. And note that there is no charge on the other side." The spectator is usually surprised that a picture of a pyramid has gathered energy. Then I would explain how it was done, with just mental pictures and flowing energy.

Occasionally, a sensitive person would feel some energy on the front, opposite the pyramid. This is just the energy the bill is naturally picking up, from being handled and carried around. To get rid of this, just run the bill between your fingers with the thought that this will remove that accidental energy. Or decide that the bill will be free of that characteristic.

If you wish to check on the effectiveness of a pyramid in helping you to meditate, you may do so without having to invest any money in one. The simplest way is to visualize, or mentally create, an energy-gathering pyramid the height of the room you are using, with your chair being at the focal point of the energy. Give the pyramid duration for as long as you wish to use it, as well as the purpose of improving your meditation. Also, visualize thanking God that your meditation was improved by its use. You can increase your reality of it by having a friend (or friends) visualize it with you.

You may wish to create a pyramid over your bed, to produce more peaceful sleep, better dreams, better memory of your dreams, or perhaps other effects, such as a more satisfactory sexual union, or possibly less snoring!

If it is true that pyramids collect energy because of expectation, then it follows that you can also stop a pyramid from collecting energy by deciding that it do so. Try it. Visualize a shield around it, to prevent it from collecting energy, and it will stop. The instant you mentally destroy the shield, and picture it being radiant again, it is.

SECTION 8.
Where the Great Pyramid Energy Came From

Since writing the preceding material on pyramids, I have been given (as inspiration) information on checking the truth concerning pyramid energy. I present it to you, so you may check it for yourself.

There were "mystery schools," or secret teaching organizations in ancient Egypt, as there are all over the world today. Some of the pyramids, at least the Gizeh

Pyramid, were used as meeting-places by these groups. There were different levels of the teachings, sometimes known as "degrees," as in some lodges of today. Upon progressing from one level or degree to the next, the student or postulant had to go through a secret sacred initiation ceremony. If he passed this, he was admitted to the next level.

Information about the use of the pyramids as initiation sites is contained in teachings of some of the esoteric groups of today.

The King's Chamber was so used in the Great Pyramid. Through the holy ceremonies and meditations of those groups, a high level of holy energy was accumulated in that area. In building up this energy, enough permanence was given to it so that it can still be felt today, but it has been changed somewhat by vibrations left by more recent visitors. Since the energy was intended to be holy, the bodies of small animals which wandered into the chamber dried up instead of spoiling. "Chapter 27," in Ostrander and Schroeder's book *Psychic Discoveries Behind the Iron Curtain*, tells about how it happened. The pyramid's shape, and its precise orientation, was blamed for the energy that was there. As a result, by intention and expectation, pyramids now collect energy! From this occurrence also came the idea of using a pyramid to dry foods without spoiling them.

Here is the proof I have been given. If you have been successful in tuning in on distant times and places, you can check it out for yourself, in this manner:

First, mentally put yourself in the King's Chamber of the Great Pyramid in present time, and note the strength and quality of the energy present. Simply decide that you are there, and feel the vibrations.

Next, decide to be there right after the pyramid was built. Don't try to do it by going back to any particular year, but just decide to be there right after it was built, and note the difference in energy. When some others and I did this, we found that it felt very ordinary, with no particular indication of special energy.

Finally, decide to move to a time when the Chamber was being used by esoteric group -- note how the energy builds up to a tremendous level!

This experiment proves to me, at least, that the *pyramid energy* is not due to any magic shape or orientation, but is *created or collected solely by mind activity in intention and expectation.* This also accounts for the wide variety of differences in the "right" way to use them, the varied effects, and the fact that some people find no reality whatsoever in pyramid power.

SECTION 9.
Reich's Orgone Energy

While we are talking about the effect of expectation on energy, we might as well make a comment or two about "*orgone,*" which is what William Reich called the creative or life energy. He constructed accumulators to gather the energy, much as pyramids are being used now. The accumulator was constructed of alternate layers of organic and inorganic materials. Reich conceived the idea that this combination would cause the orgone to be collected.

Since the energy is creative and follows thought, Reich's accumulators worked. Some of them took the form of a blanket, made of layers of wool and mental foil. Other accumulators were made in the form of a cabinet, with room for a person to sit inside. However, one had to be careful about sitting in these cabinets too long as, among other things, it often tended to make the person nervous. It seems that the problem lay in the failure to properly program the energy to *balance* the person receiving it. Evidently, the accumulators were only expected to collect energy, which they did. I believe that such mechanical accumulators do not do the proper job because the energy is not directed or balanced properly.

In our work with healing, we have seen that the energy follows the mental direction that we give it, whether the intention is to heal, to soothe and relax, to uplift, to energize, etc. The mechanical accumulator does not have this advantage. We give a person some water to quench his thirst; we do not flood him with so much water that he drowns. If I am sitting and soaking up energy for myself, when I reach a certain level, I will simply radiate the surplus to those around me who need it, or even to someone at a distance who is in need. To do the maximum amount of good, we have to put the purpose into the energy flows, and visualize the goal we wish to accomplish.

SECTION 10.
Possible Effects of Creative Energy on Particle Physics

The more we experiment with this creative energy, the more we can see that we are all using it in everyday living, no matter what we are doing, although most of us are unaware that such is the case. We are constantly creating the things we expect to happen, both good and bad, according to our needs for growth. The energy is powerful enough to move matter directly, as you will find if you experiment with my ENERGY WHEEL®, or other psychic motors.

Now, consider the scientists who are working with particle physics, or the study of sub-atomic particles. These scientists can also move matter with their minds, both consciously and subconsciously. Their theories of new particles, with particular (no pun intended) characteristics, have led to many hours of high-voltage bombardment of particles, with hopes of seeing a path in a cloud chamber which will confirm their theory. The fact is that the late well-known healer, Mrs. Olga Worrall, has been able to affect the particles in a Wilson Cloud Chamber by flowing healing energy to them, both in person and at a distance. Others have done the same thing.

Is it possible that some of these researchers may have projected their expectations into reality, and have themselves affected the particles flying through the cloud chamber, with the energy of their thoughts? The fact that some researchers have "found" new particles where others have not, although using the same techniques, suggests to me the possibility of such a psychic occurrence. It is the fulfillment of an old principle, "The experimenter is part of the experiment."

It is relatively common for an experimenter to have to discard data which did not fit his expectations, attributing his discrepancies to errors of observation. In what percentage of these incidents is psychokinesis a factor? I suspect that it happens more often than we realize, especially when the scientist has an intense desire to achieve certain results. Remember that the emotion of "desire" is a flow of the creative energy.

Herewith, I propose a question for the scientific community: What percentage of sub-atomic particles, now believed in, were "created" rather than "found"?

SECTION 11.
The Use of Crystals, Stones, Magnets, Colors, et al.

Many people are involved with the use of the above items (and many others) in bringing healing, with varying degrees of success. As with the use of pyramids, orgone collectors and other items, none of the above *is* the healing force. There is only ONE healing or Creative force, and it is in any and all places you consider or believe it to be.

For example, if you are using a crystal or a special type of stone to increase your health, or that of another, or to open up your psychic perception, or to increase your abilities in any way, it is not due to any special radiation or inherent quality of the crystal or stone. It works because *someone has assigned* certain purposes or abilities to that item. The *thoughts and expectations* of that person, and of yourself, have thus created a reality connected with the use of that item, and so it works. The other items work for the same reason. There is nothing wrong in using these methods, but I believe that we should become aware of where the real power lies. The power is in the God within you NOW.

If you feel a particular kind of energy when you hold, carry, or wear a certain crystal or stone, you will find that you can feel the same energy, undiminished in strength, by *imagining* that you are holding, carrying, or wearing it. As we have shown before, this force is not time-or-space limited. You do not have to have physical contact to achieve the desired result. This means that if you visualize wearing, holding, or being in the proximity of any crystal, stone, etc., that has certain properties in your mind, the effect can be the same as if you actually had it, unless you do not permit such happenings in your Universe. The potential to do this is in you now!

At this point, some will say that they prefer to use the physical object, and that they are not developed enough to use only the idea of the object and its assigned qualities. To those people I reply, "You *do* already have the abilities to work with the ideas alone, or you could not do it *with* the object, either!" Remember the story of Dumbo, the flying elephant, and the magic feather he carried in order to fly, or so he thought.

The same holds true for the use of magnets, colors, and other aids to healing. The magic is solely in your mind, and it is your mind that shapes the creative energy and gives reality in your universe. Do not underestimate the power of your own mind to create!

Various sources have indicated that the Atlanteans used crystals extensively to handle power, and that misuse of this power was what caused the downfall of their culture. Some of this is in the Edgar Cayce material. In considering these ideas, the thought came to me that they put too much power in the crystals (as many former Atlanteans do today), instead of using their own minds.

A crystal has no power in itself; it can only do what the mind *programs* it to do. If the minds controlling a crystal are not in accord, the results attained will be less than optimum. The Atlanteans neglected to use their minds to shape happenings, things got out of control, and thus caused their downfall.

I do not expect the foregoing information to have much of an effect upon the many people who are engaged in conducting seminars and workshops on pyramids, crystals, stones, colors, etc., even if they accept what I say as true. These people have spent far too much time and money in learning their specialties to give up the business they are doing.

SECTION 12.
How to Get a Green Thumb

Early in 1974, I was reading *The Secret Life of Plants,* by Peter Tompkins and Christopher Bird (Harper and Row, 1973), which tells of the energy fields around plants. I thought to myself, "I wonder if I could feel the energy field of a plant as I do of a person?" I passed my hand over one of our house plants, and to be sure, I could feel it. Since then, I have shown many others how to do it as easily. Try it, if you have not done so before. Sometimes I have to sensitize the person to healing energy first, then he becomes aware of what to look for.

One would suppose that the energy field over a plant would be uniform, but that is not always so. I have sometimes noticed a sharp focal point of energy, in one spot over or near a plant, which does not seem to have anything to do with the present configuration of the plant, but is there, nevertheless.

Use the same healing energy to heal your ailing plants, and to help them grow big and healthy. If I have to transplant a tree or plant, I always channel energy to it for the purpose of lessening the shock of moving it, and to ensure that the plant is going to have sufficient energy until its system is able to absorb adequate nutrition from its new surroundings. If such a plant starts to droop and wilt, visualize its' internal moisture pressure increasing until it stands up firmly, as a good, healthy plant should. You may also bless the water you give it, thus charging the water with energy. Careful tests have been made which showed that such water is *changed* by the healer's actions. I understand that there is a change in the hydrogen bonding characteristics of the water.

Some people say, "My plants grow so well because I talk to them." But it is not the talking that is responsible, nor the carbon dioxide exuded with the breath. It is the thoughts of love in the mind of the person doing the talking. *Love is the healing energy.* Admire your plants. Think good emotions at them. Emotion is the same energy.

You will recall, some time back, experiments that showed how plants grew toward a loud speaker that was playing "good" music, while other plants grew away from another speaker that was playing "hard rock" music. In these experiments, the plants are really responding to the expectations of the experimenter, and not necessarily to the music itself. Have you seen plants growing in a room where a group of musicians are accustomed to play that same music? How sick did those plants look? Quite healthy, I'll bet, if the plants were treated properly. If having music around you makes you feel good, then your plants are likely to pick up the vibrations that you radiate, and respond accordingly.

When you are in doubt whether something can be healed, remember this: We are told that every cell in the body is replaced in a seven-year cycle. In most "sick" persons, the sick cells are often replaced with new sick cells. The original pattern of the perfect cell is, however, still contained in every cell of your body! How do we know that this is true? That's easy. The entire body developed from that single first cell, didn't it? In cloning a plant, for example, a few cells are put into the proper nutrient solutions, and the few cells multiply and complete their growth into an entire new plant, exactly like the parent plant the cells came from. Orchids are grown commercially this way, I am told, to insure that they are all alike, which would not be true if they were grown from seeds, unless you completely controlled fertilization.

How are YOU replacing your sick cells? Hopefully, you will break any sickly pattern that is present, copy the original healthy pattern, and be healed. That is also the method of working with the people you are trying to help as a healer. Recreate that healthy pattern!

SECTION 13.
Improving Your Own Health
-Becoming the Source of Healing-

Whether you are a healthy person or not, it is a

good idea to set aside at least a few minutes a day for a meditative energy-gathering session, preferably at a time and place when and where you will not be disturbed. If this is impossible, do the best you can, and pray for that situation to be improved. For best results, it should be done every day. During this time you could sit or lie with your palms up, and pull in the energy for yourself, for your health, and for your attunement with God.

At this time, ask for guidance for your day's activities. Ask for answers to any particular problems you are concerned with. Be sure to thank God for giving you the correct answers as you ask for them. Then relax your mind, and just sit there accepting God's energy and guidance. Don't try to think. Just observe what thoughts come to mind. Assume that the thoughts that come after you become calm, are meaningful. It may take you a number of days or weeks to become properly calm and relaxed by following this procedure, but some improvement should be noted after a short time, and it will certainly be worthwhile to have attained this stage. It will probably help considerably to have someone else joining in with you at the same time, as the "group effect" of the two of you doing it together will give you more power. Remember that Christ said, *"Where two or more are gathered in my name, there I am, also."* This energy *is* the Christ power.

The only way you are likely to find out how this attunement method will benefit *you* is by giving it a try for a few weeks, at least. If you have trouble remembering to do it, prepare some sort of a reminder, such as a note to yourself where you will surely see it. Attune yourself faithfully for a month, at least. There should be some beneficial results for most people by this time, if you have the intention to grow and to be helped. Sometimes, however, others around you will notice the improvement first, even though you feel that nothing is happening.

In times of particular stress, it is a good idea to gather healing energy, for the purpose of calming yourself and those around you. The self should usually come first. Then, it becomes easier for you to spread energy to others. As a matter of fact, it would be an excellent idea to become totally attuned with the energy. Here is a method which could be used to attain such a goal.

Sitting or lying with your palms up, to take in energy, could be the first step to total attunement, and is a method that I recommend as being suitable for most people. It should be done every day. Do it while you are watching TV, or riding a bus, or waiting for someone. Do it while you are walking or standing. Do it any time you happen to think of it.

The next step is to visualize pulling in energy through the crown chakra, the energy spin at the top of your head. Just imagine an opening up there, and the energy entering your being. Chances are that you will immediately feel it coming in. When you can feel this quite well try doing it while you are going about your everyday business. Become conscious of absorbing the energy, while you are doing just about everything you have to do, throughout the day.

Become aware that the energy is there when you ask for it. Practice this concept until you can do it easily, on an automatic basis.

For the next step, visualize taking the energy in through your entire body, instead of just the palms or the crown chakra. The energy is all around you! This energy, or Presence, is that part of God "in Whom we live, and move, and have our being." Remember, it *is* called the Holy Spirit by some.

As you tune in on this energy or presence more and more, you may become supercharged with energy, more than you know you can use. Be sure to program it to get the best results. Decide that it shall be balanced, and give it a purpose. Make an agreement within yourself, that after your needs are supplied, any surplus will go to help someone else who is in need of it. Since the energy follows thought, such as agreement between yourself and God should automatically regulate your energy level.

The next step in this system of realization, is to consider the idea that there is, within your own body, within your own being, *right now*, as much of God's energy as there is anywhere else! Keep in mind the idea that the energy does not have to move to another place, it is just there. It is bound by neither time nor space.

Therefore, decide to BE the Source of the energy! For a starter, focus your attention on your heart chakra. This is one of the psychic centers, which is located in or near the sternum (breastbone) area, inside the body. There is a flame there, a flame of love. If you project the idea of an energy spin from one of your fingers into that area (counterclockwise as viewed from the front), you will probably feel a different feeling within you, when you are projecting it to the correct location. Once you are aware of this "flame," concentrate on expanding it.

Visualize increasing the flow of "fuel," to allow the flame to spread throughout your whole body, and fill your entire being with love. See yourself glowing with that love, and spreading it out to the whole world, while it replenishes itself. Think of yourself as a permanent channel for manifesting this Holy Presence. Reinforce this concept daily, until you can feel and *know* that this is so. You will not have to be concerned about taking in energy for healing, or any other purpose. It will always be there when you need it. Since energy follows thought, anything conceived to be a source of healing becomes that Source. It takes practice, however, to achieve that goal. Keep at it!

At times, I have told others that if they need extra energy, they can just tap into my energy field and take what they need. I have never felt any reduction of my energy when this was done, because I decided that I would automatically take in more energy on a subconscious level whenever someone tapped it.

I have met some people, serving as healing channels, who have been highly inconvenienced by someone drawing their energy while they were involved in something like driving in heavy traffic, or other critical moments, because they had told others to get energy from them when it was needed. They had not realized that replacing the "borrowed" energy could be put on an automatic basis, or even moved to a more appropriate "time" by simply deciding that it shall be so. Furthermore, your higher self knows exactly the right way to apply the borrowed energy to do the most good for the recipient.

If you are having difficulty with any particular part of the body, direct the energy to go there, with the intention to relieve the symptoms and correct the cause. Visualize the energy flowing freely into and through that part of the body, breaking the illness patterns there, and realigning the molecules in a pattern of health. See it filling with God's light and health, and see your whole body so filling with God's power that it is radiating, and lighting the entire area around you. See yourself contacting the Christ Consciousness within you, which is your own contact with God, and allowing God's healing to flow through you, unimpeded by any obstructions you have created in the past.

It is particularly important to consider your attitudes toward those around you. Do you hate anyone? Is there someone you have not forgiven? Do you blame someone else for something that has happened to you? Does someone irritate you? If your answer to any of these is yes, you are furthering any illness you may have, by keeping these feelings. When someone does irritate you, it is really the functioning of your subconscious mind that can cause an actual irritation or disease, so you are really doing it to yourself. Make sure that you consider forgiving others fully, and particularly, forgiving yourself.

There are many books which, no doubt, would be helpful in increasing your healing abilities, but one I would particularly recommend is *Who's the Matter with Me?*, by Alice Steadman (ESPress, Inc., Wash., D.C.). This book will give you clues to the possible origins of various afflictions which, when properly handled, may entirely eliminate them.

WARNING! As I was nearing the completion of this book, a very important point was brought to my attention, quite strongly. AS A HEALER, BEWARE OF NURTURING ANY NEGATIVE PICTURES IN YOUR MIND; THEY MAY MATERIALIZE MUCH MORE EASILY THAN YOU THINK!

Some time back, because of a combination of several happenings, I was dwelling on some negative possibilities. I did not realize at the time that I was giving these thoughts any emotions which would create them. (Remember that emotions are energy.) I must have done so, however, as I developed a couple of bleeding ulcers. There had been some warnings in two or three dreams, but I did not interpret them properly. When the ulcers were diagnosed, I realized how I had created them, and immediately corrected my negative thoughts. I also started to take some medication, and am now doing fine.

How were they created so easily? I am not what you would call a worrier, and am usually relaxed. Well, a healing channel has a lot more energy available than the ordinary person. It becomes easier to create the things a person wants. But since *desire* and *not wanting* (or repulsion) are both energy flows, the negative conditions are also created more easily.

Therefore, to keep the same thing from happening to you as your abilities increase, you should purge yourself of your negative thoughts by replacing them with good, positive pictures NOW, to avoid having to learn the lesson the hard way later, as I did.

SECTION 14.
How to Maintain a Strong Energy Field
-Preventing Drains-

Do you know any psychic "leeches," those who drain your energy from you when they are around you? Most of us know somebody who fits such a description. All that is necessary, is for that person to be in the same room for a while, and for some reason you seem to be drained of your energy. That is precisely what happens.

The energy apparently is absorbed on a subconscious level, and the person doing it may not be conscious that he or she is doing it. However it happens, it cannot happen without your inner self knowing, and agreeing to such an action. In other words, somewhere within yourself, you are permitting the drain to take place.

How can you break this agreement, so you will be free of this drain in the future? It can be done quite simply. Visualize your aura or energy field being intact, and free of leaks, and having the ability to prevent anyone from taking your energy unless you have consciously permitted it. You might also send that person healing energy, with the thought of his being healed of the need for absorbing others' energy. Visualize the person receiving his energy from God directly. Then rub your hands together, with the thought of cutting off your flow, as mentioned in the section on *Clearing Yourself.*

Another type of drain is possible, and this may also be corrected, if you spend the time and effort on it.

If you are involved in a number of projects, there is a tendency to worry about the condition of those you are not working on at the time. Consequently, your attention is dispersed, and your energy is scattered, making it useless for constructive work. Every time you worry, you radiate some of your energy in a destructive manner (it follows your thoughts), and thus, your energy level is always low.

Here is a way to overcome the problem. As you get ready to shelve an unfinished project before going on to another one, flow some energy into the idea of the finished project, then imagine tying up the energy and the project in a wrapper which prevents the energy from escaping. See it sort of put "on hold" until you get back to it. Then move on to your next project, which is dealt with in the same way when you are ready to leave it.

With this procedure, when you think of one of the projects "in storage," you *know* that it is still all right, and do not drain energy to it (or from it) needlessly. This will tend to increase both your energy level and your efficiency considerably.

Decide to be responsible for a high energy level, and you will see the difference it can make.

SECTION 15.
Other Types of Healing

If the creative energy is all that we say it is, we should find it useful in doing things other than attaining bodily health. And so it is. Some other types of healing are mental healing, relationship healing (see the section on *The Harmony Room*), financial healing, memory healing, attitude healing (see the section on *Subconscious Examination*), and possibly others. How about "taking-on-another's-burden" healing? A lot of people are encumbered with this affliction, believing that they are doing the other person a favor when, in reality, that person created his own problem for his own growth. Each person is ultimately responsible for his own problems. That does not mean that we should not be helpful to each other, as that is the reason we are here together! Whatever the problem, the healing technique remains essentially the same -- *see* the person *healed* as you flow the energy.

The person who is in need of financial healing could visualize money of all kinds (bills of all denominations, coins, checks, money orders, etc.) coming to him from all directions, really piling up in abundance. He should then visualize freely destroying large amounts of the money in order to make room for more to come in, but without being concerned whether more comes in to replace it or not. The idea behind this method is to get you to think in terms of abundance and plenty, instead of the scarcity that you now experience. In other words, it is intended to overcome and defuse the blocks that we have created, that keep us from receiving the money, or other things, that we have asked for.

Now here is an important factor to remember. Make sure you do this with the thought that the money is for *you*, not for another, unless that is your purpose. A friend of ours used this method, visualizing people giving her money and her thanking them for it. In a very short time she was elected treasurer of an organization. Her mental picture was fulfilled, but she had neglected to picture the money as being for her.

If *"ask and you shall receive"* is a law, as I believe it is, and if we have asked but are not receiving, then something we are doing is keeping it away from us. Picturing the blocks as having already been overcome, being able to create and destroy money, and other things, freely in our minds, will help to remove those barriers.

SECTION 16.
The Importance of Forgiveness

Forgiveness should be included in all healings. Remember, Jesus made a comment to the effect that saying "You are forgiven" is equivalent to saying "You are healed." The person who is sick should be willing to forgive others. Then he should make sure that he forgives himself. A feeling of guilt can bring on many problems.

Sometimes it is a good idea to conduct a special forgiveness ceremony, in which the subject makes it a point to forgive completely each and every participant in his past, including himself. He then decides he can accept forgiveness from God and from each person for his part in his past, and then dedicates the lessons learned, and the whole event, as an offering to God's work. Properly done, such a ceremony can leave a person with a great sense of freedom and peace.

It is important to thank God for our problems, no matter how small or how large they are, as well as our blessings. After all, each of us creates our own realities.

When we blame another, we are looking at the wrong culprit. We are the cause! In one of the old Pogo comic books, Walt Kelly says, "We have met the enemy, and he is us." As we thank God for the problem, we open ourselves to receive the solution more quickly. It is in overcoming such problems that we make our spiritual growth.

SECTION 17.
"Spirit" Healing and Spirit Guides

"Spirit" healing, as we will define it here, is the practice of inviting and allowing discarnates (spirits of departed persons, usually former doctors or else those considered to have achieved a high degree of spiritual development) to work through the person serving as the healing channel. Some of the more well-known healers in this classification were the late Tony Agpaoa, and many others in the Philippines, the late Harry Edwards and his associates in England, and the late Brazilian healer, known as Ze Arigo. Some of these healers work in trance, some work in a partial trance, and others do not. The idea is to get one's own consciousness out of the way, so that the spirit doctors can work unimpeded.

One of the ideas promoted by some of those who are doing and teaching *spirit* healing is that *only* a discarnate can correctly diagnose a patient, and intelligently direct the healing energy to heal, especially in cases of *absent* healing where the patient is "far" away. They also teach that the impulse to put the healer's hands on the body of the patient in the right place comes from the same spirit guide, instead of from the healer's own spiritual capabilities.

Another claim, made in one book I read, is that only the spirit doctors can know the "right kind" of healing energy to apply to the patient in each case. It mentioned that, as a man can direct a physical force, it takes a spirit to direct a spiritual force. It also said that the controlling mind must be a "non-physical" one.

But let us look at the facts. The mind of man is not a function of the brain. Mind is a function of the soul. So is memory, as discarnate spirits have memories and minds. Many of you know that this is truth, from your own experiences. The human mind, of a living person, does have these abilities right now, and many more. Remember that all knowledge is within all of us, without having to receive the information from discarnates. The act of losing one's body at death does not, of itself, confer wisdom and intelligence upon a spirit. *All minds are non-physical.*

Spiritual Postulations

Consider the following:

1. Man *is* a spiritual being, who just happens to inhabit a physical body from time to time. He lives by spiritual laws at the same time he lives by physical laws, because the spirit world coexists with the physical world.

2. Man's mind functions at several levels. His concepts of space and time are founded in the conscious mind, and these concepts vary according to the culture in which he is raised. His subconscious and super-conscious minds are not limited by either space or time. Therefore, with a little practice, almost any person can be taught to be aware of, and feel, and control, an energy field at a distance, without the intervention or creation of a spirit guide. This is not theory, because I have been teaching many people to do this very thing on a daily basis.

3. All matter is composed of the same basic units, through the Creative Force. All of the organs of the body were developed from that first cell at conception; the diversification of subsequent cells occurring from mental or energy patterns at each stage. All mind is really one force, as shown by the ability of one mind to tune in on another, regardless of what James Randi believes. As Edgar Cayce said, "Mind is the builder." Therefore, the *same* healing or creative energy, under proper mental direction and visualization, is utilized for healing any part of the body, or the mind itself. The important thing is to see and *know* that it is healed.

4. The controlling or operating mind mentioned in the Spirit Healing course *is* a non-physical one; that is, it is not space-time limited, whether it is the mind of a discarnate or of a "living" person. If the mind can function without a brain or a physical body (as the mind of a spirit doctor), this shows that the brain of a living person is not the source of the mind.

I want it clearly understood that I have no objection to Spirit Healing. A lot of good is being done all over the world by many dedicated men and women involved in its' practice. It is a perfectly suitable way to become a healing channel for a certain type of individual, but it is most certainly not the only way that healings can occur. The person who is properly instructed and developed can do the same things himself (as Jesus indicated), utilizing the Holy Spirit, which is available to everyone, regardless of religious faith.

We live by this energy, all of us, whether we realize it or not. Discarnate doctors do not have any more knowledge than we in the body have, as *all knowledge is within all of us!*

How does one go about becoming a spirit healer? Probably the best way is to locate one, and have him or her show you what to do. Study under that person for a while. Harry Edwards has written several books on the subject. Studying these, and applying what you learn, would be a second way. Or, you might ask in your prayers that you become a channel for the right spirit doctors to work through you. But regardless of the approach you take, keep the following in mind:

Sincerely pray that all your spirit help be *only* of the highest development. Conduct a solemn ceremony, dedicating your abilities to being of help to others. An affirmation such as this should be in your prayers every day, for best growth, no matter what you are doing.

Besides discarnate doctors, another source of spirit help in healing would be saints, and other venerated religious discarnates. Most of these have made commitments to be of service when asked, at one time or another, and I suspect that these agreements are still in force. When one has left the physical body, one is not limited in space or time, so these advanced souls are capable of being anywhere and anywhen they are needed.

The question may come up in some minds, "Suppose that such a soul were now reincarnated in another body, and the conscious mind remembers nothing of the previous life as a healer or guide. Could that person still be of help?" As far as reincarnation is concerned, it is my opinion that even those reborn in another body are still able to assist in helping another when asked, due to the timeless qualities and abilities of the soul. The soul is much greater than most of us realize -- our consciousness is such a tiny bit of the whole -- and is able to be of help regardless of what the conscious mind is doing. It is able to help many people, in various places, simultaneously. The famous stigmatist, Padre Pio, was seen at more than one place at the same time. This is sometimes called bilocation.

So choose, if you wish, the healer or saint that you seem to be attracted to, and whom you wish to work with you, and pray for attunement that you may be a good channel for that work to take place.

One weekend I was reading cards at a "psychic fair" being held at a shopping mall. At times, I was doing healing on some of the people coming to see me. A group of members (and their pastor) of a local church had set up a booth, where they were protesting that the psychic activities were "the works of the Devil." They claimed that I was not using the power of God to heal, because they didn't hear me say, "...in the name of Jesus." Their implication was that *ALL* healing is done by Jesus, and that furthermore, to achieve the healing by Jesus, one had to ask for it out loud, as though the mere words were important. A little reflection on this will show that this assumption is not so. Jesus claimed that

He was just being the channel, when He said that others could do the same things that He could, and that it was the Father in Him who was doing the works. Saint Paul said that, no matter what your "gift" is, the same Holy Spirit is the means by which it is accomplished. Furthermore, members of other religions are also healed, both in a "normal" manner and in a "miraculous" manner. People were healed before Jesus was born. After all, the healing force is Life energy itself! As far as healing with a "Name" is concerned, it is the thoughts and expectations, or the faith, of the healer and/or the subject that counts, and not the sounds caused by pronouncing anyone's name. *Thought controls energy!*

I would like to point out that you don't have to be of the same religion that the saint, doctor, or other discarnate was when living. His opinions probably changed somewhat upon passing over, anyway. All you really need is the mutual desire to be of service to others.

SECTION 18.
How You Might Acquire a Spirit Guide

Now is a good time to tell you how I acquired one of my spirit guides. On Thursday, May 18, 1978, at my weekly healing class, I unexpectedly received a baptism of the Holy Spirit through Padre Pio, and he has been one of my spirit guides ever since. Padre Pio had departed from his body almost ten years before, in September of 1968. There are many books that have been written about him and his works, and are available in libraries.

What is a baptism of the Holy Spirit? I would describe it as a flood of pure love, flowing through my whole being. As a result, all of my abilities increased, especially my healing and my psychic abilities.

Don't let anyone tell you that such a baptism means nothing if you don't speak in tongues as it happens. The important part is the flow of God's pure love. Everything else is of lesser value. If you accept it fully, it helps to clear your system of negativities, and you KNOW that God is with you!

Since that baptism, Padre Pio has been one of my spirit guides. We have smelled his roses, and otherwise felt his presence, many times at my healing class. Some people have seen him standing behind me when I have been doing counseling at psychic fairs. I have introduced him to many people for whom I have done readings, when I felt they could use his guidance. I usually do it in the following manner.

I give the person a picture of Padre Pio, and tell a little about him and his abilities. I have the person hold the picture and look at it, while imagining Padre Pio is standing behind with his hands over the person's head, and I also hold my hand over his head. I then re-create, in myself, the feeling of pure love that I experienced, and let it flow to the person. Sometimes that person will, in turn, receive a baptism of the Holy Spirit as I did, to a greater or lesser degree. (Not everybody experiences the same thing in such a baptism). I then ask the person if he would like to have Padre Pio as a spirit guide. If he says "yes," I present him with the picture, and tell him or her to read some of the books about the Padre. I also tell the person that Padre Pio always said, "Don't pray to me, pray *with* me."

If you would like to have Padre Pio as one of *your* guides, I suggest that one way is to do the following. Get a book about him, either from a library or buy one, and read about him. Then hold the book, or a picture of him, in front of you. Imagine he is with you and standing in back of you, with his hands over your head, and letting his love flow through your whole being. If you feel a good response as a result of this, mentally ask him to serve as a guide for you. You do not have to be a Catholic, the church you attend (or do not attend) may not make any difference. What does make a difference is your frame of mind, and what your aims are. It's all the same God, no matter what your church affiliation may be.

Of course, there is no guarantee that you will be guided by him, as that decision is up to him.

As an alternative, you can write to the National Center for Padre Pio, Inc., 11 N. Whitehall Rd., Norristown, PA 19403. Ask for information on how to become one of his spiritual children. They have an extensive supply of literature about Padre Pio, as well as a monthly magazine called *"The Voice of Padre Pio."*

I have other spirit guides, as well. One is a deceased brother, who crashed in an airplane at sea in 1957.

Working as a psychic, as I and many others do, we are confronted from time to time by people who firmly believe that what we are doing is the "work of the Devil." They ignore the fact that we are merely using the "gifts of the Spirit", listed in the *Bible* in *I Corinthians,*

12th Chapter. Many of us have received baptisms of the Holy Spirit, and are at peace when we are functioning as psychics, by using our gifts to help people.

One would think that all I would have to do to convince one of these doubters that I am really using God's power in my work in the psychic field would be to put my hands over the doubter's head, and let the Pure Love I have experienced flow through him so that he might feel it. That is not likely to work, however! In the first place, he would probably be afraid that I would taint him, or get control over him with my "evil power", and would not be likely to let me try it. Or, he might let me try it, but he would not accept the energy at all, and would therefore feel nothing. Furthermore, if he did let me flow the energy and accept it, he would likely feel it as an evil force, since the energy follows *his* expectations as he accepts it; unless his inner being decides it is time that he learned the truth, and accepts it as intended. Then he might be convinced.

SECTION 19.
Teaching Another to do Healing

If you are just starting to become aware of the creative energy, and how it can be used in healing and in everyday living, you are probably anxious to "show and tell" others about it as well. You would soon find out, however, that not everybody can accept the concept of such a power, which does not fit into a "scientific" category, or does not fit into their religious concept of how the Universe should be. Therefore, you should work with the energy for some time until you feel that you have pretty good control of it, so that you are able to demonstrate it at will. Show only those whom you feel can accept the ideas with an open mind, or at least without hostility.

You will probably want to teach your friends how to do healing. This, of course, involves first teaching the other person how to feel the energy. This can be done by the same methods I have been showing you, but here are some other ideas on how to increase another's ability to feel and flow energy.

1. Have the person hold both palms up, extended toward you. Hold one of your palms up to receive energy, and bring the fingers of your other hand near his fingers, about one inch away, projecting energy to his hands, one at a time. Find out what he feels, as you do this. If he cannot feel anything, wet the fingers of both hands with water, and try again. Or, try direct contact, by taking one of his hands in one of yours, and flowing energy to his hand with the intention of increasing his sensitivity to the energy. Usually, a momentary contact flow of this type boosts the sensitivity enough so the energy can be felt. Once this breakthrough is achieved, it seems that the increase in awareness is permanent. I seldom meet a person who cannot feel the energy at all, in some way, unless his personal energy is quite depleted, or he cannot or will not permit it to be a part of his Universe.

2. When you are flowing energy to him, don't just let the energy flow. *PULL* it in with your mind, and *PUSH* it out to his hands. Usually this extra push will then be felt, and he will be able to feel it later without the assist, once he has been tuned to it. If you visualize a push, it then becomes a push; if you visualize a pull, that is what you get. Try it. It's hard to describe, but quite easy to do. It *does* increase the energy being channeled.

3. Have your student hold his hands with the palms down, and tell him to observe the way his palms feel, then have him turn the palms up and feel the *difference* in energy in the palms. To give this an extra boost, mentally project extra energy to his palms as he turns them up.

4. Hold your palms out facing each other, about three inches apart, and flow energy from one hand to the other, preferably from your left hand to your right. Have the other person hold his left hand vertically above your hands, then have him lower it between yours, so now the energy is flowing through his hand to your right hand. The intention is to get him to feel the difference, as the flow passes through his hand. Have him remove his hand from between yours, and then reinsert it, to more easily feel the flow. Once he feels a difference, then repeat, only this time holding your hands further apart, say twelve inches or so, showing him that the increased distance does not diminish the flow he is feeling, or the way he feels it.

It is best to flow the energy in such a direction that it goes toward the palm of his hand rather than the back, since the palm is generally more sensitive to energy than the back of the hand.

Do not bother trying to teach someone who believes you are doing the work of the "Devil." Such a person is prevented, by the strength of his convictions, from accepting it. He does not permit it to be a reality of his personal Universe.

SECTION 20.
Working with and Attuning a Group

In order to become a better healer, it is a good idea to get involved with a group dedicated to healing. One of the effects of being in such a group, is that all of the members increase in ability, due to the creation of a "group reality." This equates to what Jesus meant, when He said that when two or more are gathered together in His name (which means with one accord), He is *there*, and thus the increase in power. The group does not have to be physically together, either. Several organizations conduct meditations and healing services at specific times of the day for their members, who may be located in all parts of the world. Each such organization has created a *power reservoir* for its members to tap and use as needed. It is possible, however, for non-members to tune in on such power structures, if the right approach is used, no matter how "secret" the organization is.

Just getting together in a group for healing does not guarantee that the group will be effective in its results. It is best to conduct some attunement ceremony to align the members, and their forces, in a uniform direction. This can be done in many ways. Here are a few ideas, which can be used to achieve the desired result in a small group, such as I usually teach. Some of these same ideas could well be used in unifying the members of prayer groups, church boards and committees, social clubs, or even business meetings, to achieve closer attunement and, consequently, wiser decisions.

Energy Circles

A common method of increasing attunement is to simply join hands in a circle. Why might this make a difference in attunement? I have a theory about what happens. First of all, the physical action of taking another person's hand is symbolic of accepting a mental and spiritual bond, as well as the physical. As the circle is completed, there is a natural energy flow that occurs, usually in a counterclockwise direction, as viewed from above. I believe this occurs due to the fact that, with most people, the energy is subconsciously accepted with the left hand and projected, or passed on, with the right hand. This can be easily reversed at will, but the natural subconscious flow is, in most people, as stated. This can be verified rather easily by experiment.

If you have a group hold hands, yourself included, without any special instructions, you will probably be able to feel the effect of the "natural" flow, which is counter-clockwise. Now, if you tell the members of the circle to consciously flow the energy out of the left hand and in with the right, you will feel the normal flow reverse to the opposite direction (clockwise), which definitely has a different feel to it. You will find that, by deciding to reverse the flow in the whole circle, you can do it easily, just assuming control over it.

The effect of this counterclockwise spin through the circle of members, is to create a vortex of energy, which tunes in to the outer spin of the crown chakra or halo; the psychic or spiritual center, which is above the head of every living person. According to Yogic teachings, this chakra, or wheel, is a complex of energy spins, which is connected with the person's consciousness of God. If you put your attention on a spot just *above* your head, you will probably feel a little dizziness, or a prickly sensation, caused by your awareness of the spin which is there.

Apparently, the large energy spin caused by the group's joining hands (and their intentions), is sort of a "super chakra," which tends to elevate the consciousness of the group for its' purposes. The activity of this composite, or group chakra, tends to modify, intensify, and refine the crown chakra of each person of the group, to sort of attune and standardize the spins, and thereby increase the total power. In electrical parlance, it could be said that the large spin is like a master oscillator in a radio transmitter, which tends to "lock in" the frequencies of the smaller, individual oscillators (the chakras). The result is an increase in attunement.

A drawback of the common circle is that, usually, the negative energy that is circled allows aches, pains and other negative conditions to be carried along with the positive to others in the circle, unless the proper programming is done to prevent this from happening. Furthermore, it is possible that the only energy that is circulated in the group is just the life energy of that group, with quite limited power. To correct this deficiency, the members of the circle should consciously decide to tune in on only *God's pure power*, and decide to transmit to the other members *only* this *pure* power. A few people do this naturally, without having to think about it, but most do not. Much depends upon the internal "agreements," or decisions, that each individual has made within his own being. Many of these agreements are non-verbal; they are just feelings, but serve as decisions nevertheless, and are therefore limitations.

Power Agreements

In the psychic field, there exist what might be called *"Power Agreements"*, or possibly "magic formulas." These are special prayers, postures, gestures, signs, configurations, etc., that have been intentionally created to have a specific result whenever someone uses them. They are used to tune in to the power reservoirs mentioned before, as well as to achieve other special effects. Some of these agreements are extremely simple, such as holding your fingers in a certain way. Notice the position of the fingers as some Yogis sit in the lotus position, with the thumbs touching a particular finger tip. This is such an agreement. Making the sign of the cross is another.

There are some power agreements that eliminate the transfer of personal discomfort with the transfer of energy, as mentioned above. They are designed to automatically circulate only the pure energy for attunement. Some were, undoubtedly, created back in antiquity. The following are five methods to form such a circle, and thus attune the group quickly.

1. Form a circle. Each person crosses his arms, with the left arm or wrist over the right one, so his right hand is extending toward his left side, in order to grasp the left hand of the person on his left. Thus the circle is formed.

As soon as the circle is formed, you will feel the power flow building up, and it will be free of all personal problems from everyone in the group. After the power builds up to the maximum, the second phase is formed; that of balancing. Simply have everyone reverse the direction of crossing the arms, so your right arm or wrist is over the left one, and everyone rejoins hands. As you do this, there is a balancing effect that occurs, a smoothing out that is hard to describe, but is easily felt by trying it. The first position is for *power*, with the *left* arm on top. The power, to be properly utilized, must be balanced properly. The second position, with the *right* arm on top, is for *balance*. If you forget which position comes first, you can easily tell just by joining hands in a circle in this manner, and observing the effect of each position. Not everyone will feel the power surge when this circle, or others like it, are formed, but most people will, unless they are hostile to it. We are not all equally sensitive. There was a time when I couldn't feel it, either. Most people, however, will be able to feel or sense that something is happening, and to feel the difference between the power and balance phases.

2. Each person sits (or stands) with his hands open, palms up. As each one pulls energy in from God, he decides to give the pure energy he is receiving to the person on his right. Hands are not joined, or touching. This energy transfer is made just by the decision to do so, and it works very well. We have often used this method in my class. In this system you are not just circulating the group energy, as each person is receiving extra energy and adding it to the circle. As a result, the power builds up quickly, and it is in balance as well.

Prayer, chanting, and singing hymns are also power agreements for attunement.

Crossing one's arms and/or legs generally tends to circulate one's energies internally, so this might be considered an isolation agreement. Therefore, when we are sitting in our healing circle, we usually sit with our hands apart and our legs uncrossed. I would like to point out that we do not have to sit in this manner to do healing, but it does help most people to tune in to a greater degree. When we are doing healing on an absent person, I usually visualize him sitting in the same manner, symbolizing his receptivity.

3. Stand or sit in a circle, with joined hands. Visualize a large vortex (spinning circle) of God's energy, the diameter of the circle or greater (counterclockwise as usual). Visualize it coming from above and enveloping the whole group, uniting, energizing, and balancing the group for best healing purposes.

4. Stand or sit in a circle. Each person puts both hands above the head of the person on his right, visualizing God's pure light coming from above through his hands, filling the person on his right with the strongest balanced flow of which he can conceive, the best flow possible for healing.

When a newcomer visits our weekly healing class for the first time, I first find out if the person has any previous knowledge about healing, to discern with what methods he or she is familiar. If he has no previous knowledge, I first show him how he can feel the energy I channel to him, and teach him to channel to me or to another of the group.

During the time that we are waiting for latecomers to arrive, we may discuss our experiences in healing, books on the subject, health changes in those sick or injured people on whom we have been working, or new ideas or techniques of healing that have occurred to us.

We experiment with different attunement methods, and we find that just the thought and visualization of joining in a "power agreement" circle works as well as doing it physically, or perhaps even better. After all, it is the thought of linking together spiritually that really does the trick. Energy follows thought! The mental effort and visualization to unite has more power to create than the physical action.

Group Healing Meditation

5. Each person visualizes light and love energy bathing the entire being of the person on his right (or the whole group, if he wishes).

You may create your own power agreements, if you so desire. They are, perhaps, most easily created by a well-attuned group. The effectiveness and permanence of a power agreement is dependent upon the reality of the power (and its limitations), as conceived and experienced by an individual, or a group, as well as the decisions about it, such as what rituals, gestures, incantations, or prayers must be used in order to contact it. The *intention* to create the agreement is of prime importance, and the power you put into it.

Back to our healing class, where we are arranged in a semicircle, with one chair in the middle, for the leader. This is usually myself, or my co-leader, or it may be one of the students who has been designated as leader for the day. After the opening ceremony, we may have a short meditation. Following this, we usually start at one end of the group, by having that person come up and sit in the chair, if he or she is in need of healing, or if healing for another is desired. I, or the alternate leader, usually lead the group in their channeling and visualization, something like the following, as I hold my hands over the head of the person in the chair:

"Now let us visualize a pure white light entering his being through the top of his head. See it cleansing out all of his negativities and hindrances, flowing them completely out of his body and mind. See him regaining full control over his body and mind -- see him able to move in any desired direction with ease, and thanking God as he does so. See him feeling the emotion of success. See his body filling with God's light and health, and being so healthy that he radiates health to those around him. See him opening the Christ Consciousness within himself, and full healing power coming through to fill his mind and body. See him being a better channel, in bringing God's blessings to others."

As I lead the group, I mentally hold the concept of all of us (both present and absent), being united in our efforts, pulling us all together as *One Force.* When we have reached agreement on the highest point of our visualization, I close off the healing by rubbing my hands together, and say, *"Thank you, Father."* The others do the same. We often work on a particular part of the body, as well as the whole being. Sometimes, there are two or three of us working with contact methods on the subject at the same time, if we are so led. One of us may be working on his feet or legs, while another is working on the neck or eyes, while the others in the circle are supporting both of us.

After we finish with the person in the "healing chair," that person then leads the group in healing the next subject, by taking my place behind the new subject, while I join the semicircle. It is a good idea to let the others have a turn at heading the group in this manner. Being at the focal point of the energy, like this, builds up the individual's confidence in what he can do, and gives him experience in handling greater amounts of energy. He may also receive more healing for himself during this time, when he is only trying to be of help to the person in the chair.

When he is through working with that subject, he goes and sits down, while the one with whom he has just finished working works with the next one in line, unless a different sequence is desired. We do not have a set pattern, but change it often. When the last one there, and the absent ones, have been taken care of, I usually sit in the chair for the last person to work with me. Then we have a closing prayer.

If the person receiving healing should start to cry, and tears flow, do not assume that you are doing something wrong. The subject is just releasing pent-up grief; just continue to give him healing until the outburst stops. If your intentions are only to be of help, every-thing that happens in the session is *supposed* to happen. You cannot make a mistake, if your intentions are right. Think of the group as being *God's* group, and not yours or anyone else's.

A well-tuned group will quite likely become psychically sensitive to each other, and simply *know* things about each other and about those being worked on. The Bible calls this the "gift of knowledge." It is common for certain members of such a group to even pick up names of departed ones relevant to the subject, who are probably spiritually present, as well as correct impressions of the physical and emotional state of the subject, whether the person is physically present or not. Occasionally, one of our class will state that it was while attending our group that they first started to pick up such information. I always encourage the members to volunteer any impression they receive, whether they are sure of it or not. Sometimes the impression is very subtle, and the person who is a beginner is likely to think that the information is from his own mind. When he finds that others are getting verification of his data, it tends to boost his ability to a great degree.

Probably the greatest advantage in working with a group is that, no matter where you go, the group in its entirety is always with you in spirit, with all the power of the whole group. All you have to do to experience this is to imagine that the group is with you, and it is. Feel the power that you normally feel at your group meetings, and it is with you immediately. Remember, neither time nor space are barriers to this force. To check this out, all you have to do is to imagine that you are with us in our healing class, and you will probably feel the power that is there, whether or not the class is still in existence at the time you are reading this. Try it!

SECTION 21.
"Calling Down" the Power of God

Some people doing healing make a big issue of "bringing down" or "calling down" the Power of God, as though God were somewhere else, and you had to work hard to get Him to come here. If we are working with a creative energy that follows thought, then such expectations will tend to be fulfilled by those who "buy" such limitations. But why make it difficult? *God's power is already here, wherever we are, all around us. Use it!*

It might be easier to produce miracles if we hold these thoughts in mind:

1. All the power that ever was, or ever will be, is here, NOW!

2. The Universe is ONE, and no part is really separate from another. Only our limited perception makes it seem divided.

3. All the Universe around you is already *within* you. The Universe within is called the microcosm, and the Universe outside of you is called the macrocosm. The hidden, or "occult", teachings say that both are the same. The Magician of the Tarot cards represents the seeker for truth (or God). When he has mastered his inner being, he has also mastered the world around him.

4. The Kingdom of Heaven is within you; and him; and me. So is the kingdom of Hell, and we *always* have our choice of which path to take.

5. *Ask, believing that you already have it, and you shall be given!*

FURTHER TIPS AND MISCELLANY

SECTION 22.
Being "Slain in the Spirit"

Several years ago, I attended a healing program conducted by the late Kathryn Kuhlman. One of the features that I observed at that meeting, was the reaction of the members of the audience who were on the stage to receive healing. As soon as she touched the person, he or she would fall backwards, unconscious, to the stage floor. One of the assistants present would catch the person, and lower him gently to the floor, to avoid any injury. The person would come back to consciousness within a very few seconds.

Some people call this event, of leaving the body in this manner, being *slain in the spirit*. There are a number of other healers who achieve the same effect, but I have seen it only once. I know the effect is not necessary to achieve healing, at least with most people. Occasionally, one of those in line will fail to lose consciousness when touched by such a healer, but most of them seem to.

I see some possible reasons why this temporary loss of consciousness might be desirable to receive healing.

1. It shows the person touched, and the spectators, that there is power in action, and that there is *something* happening.

2. It may be easier to achieve the person's healing by getting the conscious mind, and its' doubts, out of the way for a moment.

THE "GIFT" OF HEALING

I have stated before that there is a connection between healing and hypnosis, inasmuch as the same creative energy is used to give reality to the suggestions of the hypnotist. I know that many people believe that hypnotism is evil, but that simply is not true. Hypnotism is a useful tool. Any tool may be used for either constructive or destructive purposes, so it all depends upon the *intentions* of both the hypnotist and the subject, and the manner in which it is used.

When a hypnotist does a stage performance, he often uses various visual and verbal ploys to increase his percentage of success. He might tell the audience in his introduction that they are going to see some of the fastest hypnosis that they have ever seen. If he has an easily-hypnotized person for his first subject, all that follow will be better subjects than if the first one is difficult. The success of the first subject acts as a suggestion on the others to follow, and they tend to *expect* to react in the same manner. Sometimes a "plant" is used, a person who has been hypnotized before, and therefore "goes under" very easily and quickly. Those who follow expect the same reaction, if only on a subconscious level, and so their expectations are generally realized.

It seems to me that the situation with a healer before a group is somewhat analogous with the rapid hypnosis pattern. That is, when the healer touches the first in line and he "passes out," the subsequent people in line expect to react in the same way, and so they do. Most people are quite susceptible to suggestions of this type. I know, as I first did hypnosis in 1934, when I was a Junior in high school.

I do not claim that the healer creates the unconsciousness deliberately, although he certainly expects it to happen, and so it usually does.

I do not know if I would "pass out" if such a healer laid a hand on me. So far, I have not met such a healer. Perhaps some day I shall know!

SECTION 23.
Getting Rid of Negative or "Evil" Forces Around You

Is this world we live in a "World of God," or a "World of the Devil?" Opinion is quite divided on this question, with both sides often quoting various scriptures to support their beliefs. In reality, the choice is ours individually.

I would like to call to your attention one of the statements made by Edgar Cayce, who said: "Mind is the builder." The things that happen to us are created by ourselves, whether they are "good" or "evil" happenings, so we *always* have a choice as to what expectations we nurture and the images we create with our minds. Jesus once said, "Know ye not that ye are gods?"

In the "beginning," God created the heavens and the earth, and He said that it is *good*. Now God is not limited, as we are, in our consciousness of time, so it is *still* good, forever. No other force can "take over." But we are *given* free will. If you are looking for evil, you tend to find it. If you are looking for good (or God), you will tend to find that as well.

Perhaps it would be a good idea to check on the lives of some great people who have undergone an "illumination," or "cosmic consciousness," experience. Such a study has already been made, many years ago. The researcher was an M.D., and his name was Richard Maurice Bucke. The book is entitled *Cosmic Consciousness*, published by University Books, Inc., Library of Congress # 61-11100. Mr. Bucke had an *illumination* experience, which transformed and elevated his being.

He checked histories and found that quite a number of people had had similar experiences, including Saul (Paul), Dante, Spinoza, Whitman, and others. Bucke found that there were similarities in the experiences each one had, as he received the illumination. Here are some:

1. A subjective light filled the person, who in some cases thought, at first, that the light was external.

2. An elevation of the morals of the person.

3. An illumination of the intellect: *knowing* many things, immediately, that could not be learned from books.

4. A sense of immortality.

5. Loss of the fear of death.

6. The loss of the sense of **sin.**

Bucke tells of his personal experience. Among other things, in a flash he *knew* that the whole Universe is *alive,* that the soul of man is Immortal, that the Universe is constructed such that: *"All things work together for the good of each and all, that the foundation principle of the world is what we call love, and that the happiness of everyone is, in the long run, absolutely certain."*

The intensity and thoroughness of the illumination experience varies with the individual. One factor, I believe, is the degree of willingness to discard one's old patterns of belief; to consider expanding one's consciousness to accept a broader concept of God's Universe. I recommend reading the book.

God is often referred to as Light, Life, and Love. Therefore, one of the best ways to clear your surroundings of "evil" or negative influences is to study the *23rd Psalm*, and realize that it promises you protection wherever you go, if you accept it. Then, think of yourself as His Light, Life, and Love, manifest within your own being, and lighting the area around you wherever you go, as well as going to all those you encounter. Purify your own thoughts. Remember, no darkness can exist where there is God's Holy Light.

SECTION 24.
Be Sure to Clear Yourself

Clearing yourself properly, after doing healing on a person, is so important that it bears repeating, and special attention. As you complete your healing application, always rub your hands together or shake them to signify the end, to cut off the flows, both inflow and outflow. In this way you can do healings all day, and still have a good buildup of personal energy.

If you should identify with the patient, in order to

tell what is wrong with him, be sure to reaffirm your own identity when you are through. If you do not feel sufficiently released by rubbing your hands together, wash your hands in cold water, with intent to cleanse and separate you from the patient.

Be sure to let go of your healing visualization. The picture has to be released from the conscious mind to get to the God-mind. Once you complete the healing, put it out of your mind; think of something else.

SECTION 25.
Success or Failure?

It is difficult to evaluate the results of anyone's efforts to bring healing to a sick or injured person, regardless of the type of treatment. Once in a while, the healing may be instantaneous and certain, and you will know that the problem is gone. Sometimes the effects will be obvious, but the permanence will be questionable. At other times other circumstances will prevail, or the attempt to heal will seem to be a total failure. Note that I said, "seem to be," for all the effects of our efforts are not usually seen at once. Healing of mental patterns may take a long time, with the body changes following these mental changes more slowly. Each case is different.

Most healers say that they don't know why some are healed and some are not. But that holds true for any method of healing, doesn't it? There are no guarantees. If it is true that we create our own reality, then the answer truly lies in the patient, in every case. A person will not be healed until he is ready to be healed; healing cannot be forced. That readiness must come from deep within the inner self, and is seldom the same as expressed by the conscious mind. The conscious mind may be saying, "Yes, Lord, I'm ready to be healed. Heal me!," while the deep inner self may be saying, "Not yet! I must first learn how my attitudes and actions are affecting others, and must suffer a while longer, until my lesson is well learned."

The soul is capable of changing the body instantly, if the attunement is sufficient. Most of the time, however, the progress is slower, and no healing may be visible for a while. Nevertheless, some activity may be in process on a deep level.

Some patients go to one healer after another, and nothing seems to come of it. I suspect the parting thought is often something like, "It didn't work. He is not as good as his publicity says he is." It makes more sense to me, though, to conceive that each of those attempts was a necessary step that had to be taken in the progress of that patient. There was some benefit, or aspect of each healing attempt, that would fit into the total pattern of healing that was necessary for that person.

The foregoing makes more sense, when we consider the viewpoint that the Universe is perfect, and that everything is exactly where it is supposed to be at this time. Note carefully the following: This does not mean that you are supposed to remain as sick, tomorrow, as you are today. Instead, do something today to help create a healthier you for tomorrow! Start becoming more aware of the creative energy, and put it to work in your thoughts of yourself and others! Look for holding patterns that tend to keep you as you are.

Do not be discouraged if you see no miraculous, instant healings occur. Your greatest value as a healing channel may be in elevating your patients to a higher level of responsibility for their own health, rather than the production of instant miracles. When I give a person a healing, I usually have him turn his palms upward and pull energy in. I also tell him what I am visualizing, as I work on him. I tell him to sit thus every day, and program the energy for his needs of the day. This should help him to alter his mental patterns to a healthier outlook, if he is ready to take responsibility for his health.

Responsibility for Health

Some persons are not ready to take responsibility for improving their health. They may tell you, "That's what I have a doctor for. That's his job." So they put their faith in medicines and surgery only, instead of looking at the real causes of illness. They seldom know how it feels to be healthy. Others may not use the slightest amount of common sense in taking care of themselves, seemingly programmed for "self-destruct."

Some persons do not want to get better. If they got well, they would be expected to do certain things, to take on various responsibilities which they would rather not. Getting sick is one way to control the people around you, who would have to cater to your wants and needs. If the patient you are working on is not ready to relinquish that control, you are either not likely to heal him, or he will not stay healed very long, but will recreate his illness, or another as its substitute.

Because of this tendency, it is a good idea to visualize the patient as so enjoying his healing that he is willing to discard his old control patterns, and be healthy.

You will probably find that there will be times when a person is healed of one illness while you are trying to bring healing for another condition. One reason for this is that not all illnesses are caused by the same factors. The patient may be ready for healing his ulcers, but not his back, because the two conditions do not have the same cause. Perhaps the ulcers may be the result of hating his boss or his job, while his bad back may be due to his having to support some relative who lives with him. Suppose he switches to a job he likes? His ulcers may go, but his other problem would still be with him. Be thankful for whatever healings do occur.

Do the best that you can, and don't take responsibility for any so-called "failures" you have. Remember that the patient is creating his own Universe just as you are creating yours. In addition, that failure may be part of a still greater healing, yet to come in the life of that individual.

Just think of what would happen if most people

realized that they create their own circumstances, whether they are good or bad. Medical expenses would drop considerably, because malpractice insurance would no longer be necessary!

When you are serving as a healing channel, you have many questions directed at you by those whose concepts are very limited. For example, "Who is doing the healing? Is it God or Satan? How do you know which one it is?" I try to get across the idea that there is only One Source of healing in the Universe, and that is God, or the Holy Spirit, or the Christ Force, or Love, no matter what other names we may give to it because of our education or miseducation. *All* forces in this Universe, including the Holy Spirit, can be used either for constructive or destructive purposes. The choice is ours. Each person is held responsible for how he uses that force, as the force we send out to others will be returned to us. Remember, the microcosm is also the macrocosm, so that what you do seemingly to another, you are really doing to yourself. This is the wisdom behind the *Golden Rule.*

Do not refuse to give healing to someone because "He's suffering because it's his karma." The healing will be refused by his inner being if he is not through using the illness for his development. At least you will have the satisfaction of having tried to help him.

In a field such as healing, where the law is, *"Ask and you shall receive,"* there can be no complete books or other complete instructions on the subject. As creative energy is applied to an idea concerning a new method of healing, it becomes a valid method in reality. Energy follows thought! This leads to the creation of many, different methods, and will continue to do so. Furthermore, as you apply whatever abilities you have to any method, you are always given more.

I have attempted to give the basic methods involved in the healing process, without adding too much in the way of gimmicks, "window dressing," or unnecessary frills.

The following chapter on *Healing Past Lives* may turn out to be the most useful to many people, since it will tend to prove that we ARE Eternal Beings, and that we reap what we sow!

CHAPTER SEVEN
Healing Past Lives

CHAPTER SEVEN
Healing Past Lives
SECTION 1.

For many years, there has been much controversy regarding the reality of reincarnation or "past lives." This was brought closer to the public when a hypnotist, Morey Bernstein, brought forth a book about "Bridey Murphy" as a result of the hypnotic regression of a housewife to a past life in Ireland. Since then, many other people have been investigating the reality of past-life memories in a number of ways. Some children have come up with natural memories of who they were and what they did in previous lives.

Some researchers use either hypnosis or meditative techniques to draw out the data from the subconscious mind. Study of one's dreams is also useful. Now, many past-life seminars are being held around the country by various individuals and organizations.

I believe (and know) that reincarnation is real. I have glimpses of some of my past lives, from time to time, in my dreams. I am convinced that we are eternal beings. If we ever do have eternal life, we have always had it, since the symbol of eternity is a circle or ring. All souls were created in the *beginning*, whatever that means. The term "old soul" refers to a person who seems to have carried to the present life more of the wisdom from his past lives than the ordinary person does. Our conscious concept of "time" is very limited, and these concepts vary from one culture to another.

We speak of "holistic" healing, do we not? If we are doing healing in a truly holistic manner (meaning to consider the whole person), then we must consider the entire time extension of the person, including his past lifetimes. Each person is, today, the result of his entire past, and all knowledge of the past within each of us.

I have been involved in doing past-life regressions for several years. I used hypnosis in doing the first one. Later on, I learned the basic technique taught here, which in my estimation is much easier to use, and is not a trance state. If the subject tends to go into trance, I get him out of it. It is an awareness technique, which I refer to as a "level shift." I believe it works more universally than does hypnosis. The subject can open his eyes at any time, and can even discuss the things he is looking at, then close them again and continue to experience the past data. An occasional subject will even do the entire regression with his eyes open.

I have observed that, in a number of regressions I have read about or seen others conduct, the subject has benefited somewhat by the information brought forth from the past; but in only some of the cases. Merely understanding what sort of an occurrence in the past has caused a present-life situation is usually not sufficient to heal the condition. I sensed that there must be ways of improving the benefits derived, and I was inspired to modify the basic awareness technique to achieve that goal. As you use this method, you be the judge of whether or not my goal has been achieved.

It is not important to me whether the subject can verify a past life through old records or tombstones. Two close friends of mine, however, a man and wife, have been regressed by this system many times, and they have found that they are in agreement concerning the information they have uncovered in the past lives when they were together.

My most important question is whether the subject has benefited by the experience or not. In just about every instance, when I have finished the session, the subject immediately felt better. We usually find instant changes for the better, in one way or another. Consider this: *Healing the past can heal the present, and therefore the future!*

I am indebted to a man named William Swygard for the basic technique I use. Years ago, he had a letter in the "Reader's Department" of *FATE Magazine*. (*FATE* is published monthly by Llewellyn Publications, 213 E. Fourth, St. Paul, MN 55101. It is the best in its field.) In the letter, he stated that he had a technique he called *"Multi-Level Awareness,"* which he would send free to anyone who sent a stamped self-addressed envelope to him and requested a copy. I sent for one and tried it out, and it worked. It was intended to enable anyone to explore his own past lives, and thus realize more of his own being, and the Universe.

Quite some time later, I noticed an ad he had placed in FATE, telling of three booklets he had published, called *"Awareness Techniques," books I, II, and III, and I* ordered them. The *Multi-Level System* is in *Book I*. I must add that the only information that I could use from the 3 books, was the same information that I had already received free. The address given at that time was "Awareness Techniques, P.O. Box 49, Wellesley Hills, MA 02181."

Since my purpose is to heal the past, I made some changes in the handling, and the method given here is the result.

A few years ago, I was reading Tarot cards at a psychic fair in the Chicago area. It was in December, and there was a blizzard in progress, so there were very few customers attending. Consequently, the readers were not busy at all.

Some of us were standing around talking, including the lady who was managing the fair. I mentioned the regression technique to her, and offered to conduct her in a past-life experience. She agreed, so while we were standing there, I conducted her through the process. She was quite impressed by the simplicity and success of the method. She said to me, "Why don't you do this at these psychic fairs? No one else is doing it."

After a short deliberation I decided that I would do so, and have been doing it ever since, in addition to my Tarot counseling. I also do private regressions at home. I teach every person with whom I work some of the techniques for healing, and for creating desirable changes in his or her life.

Any system you might use for regression will be more fruitful by channeling healing energy to the subject as you work with him. It will improve his concentration, and ability to contact the important data. Mental images will be sharpened, and your rapport will be much better. You, yourself, will get more accurate impressions of what he is looking at, and will know better which questions should be asked. I always have the subject turn his palms up, in the receptive mode. If I am at a psychic fair sitting at a table, I extend my own hands in a similar manner and maintain a touch of my fingers to his. At some other times I do not touch him, such as when we are sitting in chairs across the room from each other. In that case we both sit with upturned palms. Either method may be used.

Each session should be preceded by agreeing upon a goal. If it is the subject's first time, I usually say something like this: "Let's ask that you be presented with knowledge of the past life that is the most important to your being at this time, from which you will benefit the most." The reason for this choice is that the past-life data which is affecting the subject is just below the conscious level. This is similar to a post-hypnotic suggestion, since it is "forgotten," but still affecting the person.

In explanation of the above, a hypnotist might give a suggestion to his hypnotized subject such as this:

"When I awaken you, every time I touch my tie, you will take off a shoe. You will not realize why you are doing it. You will forget what I have told you, but every time I touch my tie you will remove your shoe. Now, when I count to five, you will be wide awake and refreshed. One, two, three, four, five! Wide

awake!" The subject opens his eyes and remembers nothing. When the clue of touching the tie is done, the subject may feel that something is in his shoe, so he takes it off and checks it, then puts it back on. When the clue is given again, he might say that his foot feels hot, and takes it off again. He may make a different excuse every time. If he should suddenly connect the clue to his shoe removal and realize why he is responding in that manner, then the post-hypnotic suggestion loses its effectiveness, unless he consciously chooses to follow it again. In other words, by bringing the buried data to the consciousness, it can no longer affect the person, unless he chooses to be affected.

The data from the past life acts in the same manner. Once brought to the conscious level, its power to affect you is gone. Only the things hidden in the subconscious can be aberrative.

It should be understood that this is a non-hypnotic technique, which is and under the control of the subject at all times.

One of the books on working with past lives warns you to stay away from contacting those past lives with a lot of pain or heavy emotions, as they may be too much for the subject to handle. Our intention here, however, is to *handle and release* all trauma that brought forth. With the use of the healing energy from the conductor, or spirit guides, or the healing intentions and abilities of a person working alone, everything that comes up can be safely handled, and the power drained from it by forgiveness. *All* the trauma in our entire beings *must* be dealt with eventually. The sooner these "bundles of energy" are released, the more freely we can function in everyday living. Once released, they need never be handled again.

It is not necessary to feel again all of the pain, or heavy emotion, that was present originally. The only thing of which you must be aware is that the pain or emotion was there, and do the forgiveness ceremony as presented here. If your subject is reluctant to forgive himself in a particular lifetime wherein he has wronged another, point out that each person creates his or her own circumstances, including the wrongdoings that others do to him.

A person only hurts himself by refusing to forgive. Do not leave a past life unforgiven. If the law is: *"Ask, and it shall be given,"* then there are no unforgivable sins! Remind the subject that he has nothing to lose, and everything to gain, by forgiving the past.

SECTION 2.
The Thirteen-Step Regression Technique

Once you have decided upon the goal, tell your subject the following. Instructions to you, the operator, are in parentheses:

1. *"Close your eyes. This technique is an expansion method, to aid you in moving through time and space without taking your physical body. Follow to the best of your ability. Project yourself up, through the top of your head, and become a few inches taller. Tell me when you have achieved this, by saying 'Okay' or nodding."* (Wait for the signal). *"Now, go back to normal size and tell me when you have done so...Now repeat, making yourself a foot taller...Go back to normal size.* (If the subject has difficulty in projecting up, create an energy pull with a hand above his head, and visualize it pulling him up higher. If he still has difficulty, tell him to do it to the best of his ability, and proceed. Have him project up and return three or four times in this manner.) *Remember that when your physical body grew larger, your inner spirit expanded in this manner to fit the size of your body. We are just carrying that a step further.*

2. *"Now go to the other end, and project yourself down through your feet, and become taller in the same manner. Tell me when you achieve it... Go back to normal size...*(This is also done three or four times. If difficulty is again encountered, create a pull with your hand, and visualize it being below his feet, to pull it out. Just imagine it being there below his feet.)

3. *"Now, I want you to expand through your head, feet, arms, legs, and the whole body. Expand in all directions -- just blow up like one of those balloons they use in parades, and tell me when you achieve this.*

Now go quickly, and stand in front of a house you used to live in, when you were younger in the present life. Describe it to me somewhat, and tell me where it is located. Do you have a clear view of it?... (If not, tell him to imagine himself focusing the picture more clearly, as one would do with a camera. After he describes the place briefly, continue.)

4. *"Now, I want you to be up on the roof of the building, and look down from there. Don't worry, you can't fall down. Note how much farther you can see from there.*

5. *"Now, be about 500 feet high in the air above the house, and observe the whole area below you. What sort of a day is it? If it is a cloudy day, change it to a clear, sunny day. What time of the year is it? ...Now move to a cloudy day, right after a rain has stopped. Smell the cleaned air. See the water* *running off the roof, and the puddles on the ground...Now, go to a night scene, a clear but dark night. Some stars are visible overhead, and light is streaming from windows. Other lights are probably visible as well...Now change to a night with a full moon, and see how beautiful the scene below is by the reflected moonlight...Now go back to a sunny day.*

6. *"Leave that house, and rise higher in the air above the earth, and expand still more. In a moment, I am going to have you come back to the earth, but as you come down you will be moving back in time to a time when you lived before, with a different body and, probably, a different name. You will go to the past lifetime which is the most important to you right now...As you come down to the earth and your feet touch the ground, gently but firmly, the earth which has been spinning below you will stop at just the right geographical location where the past life occurred. You will be there and then, complete with the memories and activities of that lifetime. Let me know when your feet touch the ground.*

7. *"Look down. What are you wearing on your feet, or are you barefoot? How are you dressed? Are you male or female? How old are you?* (If the subject does not know, tell him to give you a number, the first one that comes to mind. This is his correct age at that point) *Do you get any impression of what your name is? What do they call you?* (If no name comes to mind, just proceed.) *What kind of a location are you in? Is it sandy, rocky, near water, trees, a town or city?* (Have him describe the area.)

8. *"Now it is time to go to your home, the place where you live. What sort of a place is it? Go in and see how your home feels to you. Does anyone else live there with you? Is your mother there? If so, consider her personality. Is it the same, or similar, to your present mother, or is it different? If* *she seems the same or similar, it is probably the same entity. Since there is sometimes a reversal of roles, it could even be your present father or another relative. Use the impression that seems right to you. You are able to quickly scan the lifetime either, forward or backward, to get the data you seek. If your mother is not visible at this point in the past life, move earlier to a time when you are together, to check on her personality and compare with today's mother. Check on the identity of your father in the same manner ... Do you have any brothers or sisters? Can you identify them with today's family or relatives?* (You can also check for close friends and other relatives.) *Also look for people with whom you had relationship problems, as it is possible they are still giving you problems today.*

9. *"What kind of work do you do? What special skills do you have? What things do you like to do, when you are not busy working? Which of these abilities, or pleasures, are still present in today's lifetime? Some of these former skills may be things you have always had a desire to do. If so, perhaps you can recapture those former skills by further investigation of this past life.*

10. *"How is your health in that life? Do you have any accidents or injuries? If so, see how they were caused and decide to forgive all such events totally.*

11. *"Look for decisions, made then, that could interfere with what you are doing in your present life, such as 'I'll always do this,' or 'I'll never do that.'* (If you locate such limiting decisions, point out that now he can negate or cancel these decisions, and make new ones to change his future. This is important! Also, check to see if the subject had a "Oneness" experience of God's presence, or find out what his highest emotional experience was. Such an elevating occurrence can be easily brought up to present time, to remember and uplift when things in the present are dragging him down.)

12. *"Now, move to the end of the lifetime, and see how you died. How old were you? If you do not know how it happened, be there just before it happened, and observe how it occurred. What was the immediate cause of death? Where do you feel it in your body? Was the death quick or lingering?*

13. *"Now be at the point where you have left the body in death, and you are looking at the lifeless body before you. This is the most important part. I want you to decide to forgive totally everybody who ever did anything to you, or tried to, or wanted to, during the entire lifetime, including the death experience... Have you done that? Now, decide to forgive yourself totally for everything you ever did to everyone else, or tried to, or wanted to, during that life. Okay? Now, decide to accept ALL the events of the lifetime, both positive and negative, as blessings, because the lessons learned from them helped you become the wonderful person you are today. Finally, if there are any residues of physical, mental or emotional problems, they are to be dumped in that still form you have just left, and your spirit is free!"* (Have the subject open his eyes.)

At this point, ask the subject if he or she suddenly feels lighter. This has happened in every case I have worked on. This shows us that the subject has gotten rid of something that had been carried to present time, and is now gone!

Some may wonder why a simple forgiveness should bring healing. The *Bible* indicates that Jesus often said, "Your sins are forgiven," and the person was healed. When asked about this, Jesus said something like this: "Which is easier to say, 'You are healed,' or 'Your sins are forgiven'?" They are equivalent.

SECTION 3.
Some Examples of Healings

The proof of the previous statement, that something is changed, *is* in the results. For example, suppose the subject had died from drowning. This usually results in a fear of water (even in taking a bath), and breathing difficulties. At the termination of such a session, I ask the subject to breathe deeply, and easier breathing is usually claimed. The loss of the fear of water usually occurs; I have been told this later by the subject.

Here is another quick result. I conducted a regression on a young man. He had had a pain, for a long time, in the cervical area of the spine. The past life he remembered was one when he was beheaded by means of a guillotine. That was the source of his pain in the neck, because the pain disappeared, and is still gone after a couple of years! I hear from him every once in a while, as we are now good friends.

A young lady who came to me told me that she couldn't stand to have anyone touch her neck. She came up with a lifetime when she had been choked to death. After we had finished the session, I reached over to her and put my hands on her neck, and she just smiled at me! The fear pattern was gone.

A young man came to me, at a psychic fair, for a past life conduction. He told me he was an epileptic. He went back to a past life when he was knocked unconscious. I do not recall the details of how it happened, but I believe he died while he was still unconscious. We did the forgiveness ceremony as usual. This session was held on November 1st of that year. On February 14th of the following year, I was at another psychic fair, and a lady approached me. With tears in her eyes, she said, "I am so happy to finally see you again, and to give you the good news. Because of your working with my grandson last Fall, he is healed of his epilepsy! He had an EEG following that, and it showed that he is cleared of the problem!" Of course, I was extremely happy to get the news. Her grandson was there with her. He is quite psychic himself.

That is not the end of the story. I always tell the subject that, once he has learned the technique, he can take himself back, and does not need me to do it any more. My wife and I were attending an 82nd birthday party, given for a well-known medium, the next month, and his grandmother was there to help celebrate. My wife was talking with her, when she told my wife that her grandson had had about 30 food allergies, but by using the method I used on him, he took himself back to some past lives and got rid of the allergies! I have talked to her several times since then, and he is doing fine.

You don't have to be with the subject to take him back. A young lady called me on the phone, and told me that she had a very bad back problem. I suspected it stemmed from a past life, and I got the impression it was caused by falling off a horse. I asked her if she wanted to make an appointment to come to me, but she said that she had no car. I suggested that, since we were pretty well in tune on the phone, she could call me the following evening at a time when we would both be free, and she agreed. When she called, I regressed her to a life wherein she was an Arab man. The man whom she was currently dating in present time, was a girl in the past life. In the episode that appeared, she (as the man) began drinking, and picked up the girl, and they rode off together on his horse to have some fun. Apparently the girl objected. At that point I had the sudden thought, "I'll bet there's a stabbing here." Right after I thought that, she said, "I didn't see that dagger at first." As the man, "he" had a dagger at his waist. The girl riding behind him took it, and stabbed him in the back, and *then* the fall from the horse occurred, and the man (she) died. We completed the session in about 20 minutes.

Afterwards she asked, "Do you think I'll ever be able to stop taking these drugs?" I answered that she probably would. About a week later, I received a nice note from her, saying that the back problem was entirely gone. Her doctor told her he didn't understand how such a serious problem could suddenly disappear all by itself, but she did not tell him how it was done. I have seen her a few times since, and she is healed.

An overweight young man came to me for a past life conduction. He wanted to find out why he was so heavy in this life. He went back to pioneer days, and a trip west. He and the other children were always admonished, "Eat more food, while it is available. You don't know when you will get you next meal." They always stuffed themselves when they could, and the pattern was set. Once aware of the pattern, he was no longer compelled to follow it.

SECTION 4.
The Effect of the Past
on Today's Relationships

Someone has said that we return to be together, again and again, for two reasons -- love and hate; and that all hates must eventually be changed to love. Everything that we project to another must eventually return to us, so it behooves us to do something about bad relationships as soon as possible, for our own benefit. If two people in a past life had relationship problems, and they were never resolved, then chances are that if they are drawn together again in this life, they are being given another chance to rectify their differences. An instant like, or an instant dislike of another, is often an indication that the two of them have known each other before. The circumstances connected with the relationship can be checked with this technique.

To do so, take your subject (or yourself, if you wish to check your relationship with another), to the stage in the regression where he is expanded, high above the spinning earth. As he comes down while moving back in time, have him focus on going to the origin of the relationship problem when the two of them were together, or to the first time they met, whichever is appropriate to your goal. This will draw him to the proper past life. Once there, direct the subject to move to the relationship, and find out the nature of the problem. Get all the information you feel is important, and then move to the death scene. Do the forgiveness ceremony as usual. This often makes instant improvements in the present-time relationship. The reason for the instant change is that some aspect of the other person's soul is aware of the forgiveness and release by your subject, at the same time that it happens, regardless of where the other person might be! As a result, the improvement will usually be evident the next time they are together, or when they next communicate with each other.

SECTION 5.
Supplementary Instructions for the Regression Steps

In the following comments, to the numbers referred to indicate the regression steps.

3. If the subject has always lived in the same house, that's all right; use that house.

5(a). At a psychic fair in Rockford, Illinois a few years ago, I was directing a man from Wisconsin to be in the air above the farm where he had been raised, and he said, "Oh, I've been up here many times." I asked him how that could be, and he said, "I used to astrally project when I was young."

6(a). Sometimes the subject comes down to the same house he was just at in the present life. When that happens, it usually indicates an important occurrence there which is in need of healing. Possibly the death of a loved one happened there. If that is the case, point out that that person created his own life and death at that time. His spirit did not *go* anywhere; his or her love is still present within the subject. Have him look within his *own being* and find that love. Have him forgive the loved one for leaving his physical body at that time (since his life plan was completed), and forgive himself for blaming that person for leaving in death. Then direct him to expand and be high above the earth again, and proceed as before.

6(b). If the subject cannot come all the way to the ground, have him go back to the same house and follow 6(a) above.

6(c). Sometimes the subject cannot come down to the earth, but goes to a time between lives, where a barrier has been created to prevent his going back to a former life, until he is able to handle it properly. If this occurs, and you can locate the block and the decisions that set it up, you may be able to cancel or defuse the block, and thus proceed as before. However, realize that not *every* person is ready to look at a past life.

7. If the subject does not know what he is wearing, coax him. Tell him to make something up, the first thing that comes to mind. Use that impulse as truth, and proceed. The easiest thing to make up, is that which is just below the consciousness!

If you are psychically picking up the information needed, give him an occasional clue, if it seems appropriate. It will likely help him to tune in more accurately. You may occasionally pick up his name in the past life.

8(a). Suppose the subject had close relatives or friends in the former life, who cannot be located in the present one. Have him look within himself, to find if he can detect that person's presence and love in his own being. If he can, it is possible that that loving entity is serving as one of the subject's spirit guides. This happens quite often. As a matter of fact, my brother Ronald, who died in 1957 on his way to Japan, has been one of my spirit guides for several years. It is common for close people to take turns guiding each other in subsequent lives, because of the love between them. *Nobody is ever lost!*

8(b). In examining the past life of your subject, you may sometimes experience a strange feeling as you are discussing one of the characters, and recognize that that character is YOU! You will both recognize it almost simultaneously. As you do, the rapport between you goes sky-high! It's a great feeling, as it happens to me every once in a while. It goes to prove that former friends tend to meet again and again, and tend to reincarnate in the same geographical areas. When this happens to you, you'll know what I mean!

10. Accidents or injuries located can either be forgiven immediately, or deferred until the end of the session, when everything is covered. Use your intuition on this. If the event is quite traumatic, it is probably best to do the forgiveness for this event *before* proceeding.

If the emotions present are too strong to experience directly, have the subject see what happens as if it were happening to someone else. This will discharge enough of the trauma so that it can then be experienced as himself, and thus fully discharged and forgiven. In most cases, the subject will have had problems with a part of the body that was injured in that life, and the present body will often be healed by the forgiveness of the incident of the past life. Not all such injuries of the past are manifested in the present life, but the potential for its restimulation is still there. Forgiveness of the past episode, so that the subject feels lighter, indicates that the probability of a problem in that area of the body has been removed, unless there has been another injury in the same part of the body in a lifetime previous to that one. If you suspect that this might be the case, check by seeing if such a previous injury does exist.

Doing an additional regression is very easy. Just have the subject be expanded high above the earth, and come down with the intent to locate a previous life with the earliest injury in that area of the body. If there is one, forgive the entire lifetime as usual.

13(a). If the subject cannot see his lifeless body before him, such as when the body is destroyed at death, have him make up such a picture, and proceed with the forgiveness ceremony.

13(b). After the forgiveness, you can ask the subject if he was aware of any spirit guides around him. Occasionally you will find that to be the case. Often, loved ones who have passed on will be there to greet and guide the subject.

SECTION 6.
Other Considerations

Sometimes, when the cause of a certain problem is sought, it will be found in the present life. If so, go through the events connected with the problem to discharge the trauma, then do a forgiveness of this life, up to the present.

We know, from our viewpoint as healers, that *our intention* is an important factor in the outcome. Since, in this regression, the intention is to come up with the truths that will help the subject, then we must accept what the subject comes up with as pertinent, even though we may at first think that it is purely his imagination. It usually turns out to be an important part of the process.

One time while I was working with a young man, as he was considering something he was looking at within himself, his body suddenly jerked. "What happened?" I asked, He replied, "I just realized this is real!"

Occasionally a subject will be reluctant to forgive someone who has wronged him in the past life during the closing ceremony. Point out to him that he created whatever happened to himself, and should therefore accept responsibility for it. Tell him that he will only hurt and limit himself by refusing to forgive other persons. In forgiving others, he cleanses himself. Remember that Jesus said, "Forgive them, Father, for they know not what they do."

It is said that, when Mahatma Gandhi was shot, he gave the sign of forgiveness as he dropped, thus eliminating the need to be reincarnated to settle the score with the assassin.

There are probably some critics who will insist that the material that comes to the mind of the subject is merely the result of suggestion, a fabrication of his mind. I do not give suggestions to the subject, however, as I would if I were using hypnosis. You see, as I am somewhat skilled at hypnosis, as well as a healing channel, a statement becomes a suggestion only when I intend it to be a suggestion. If I intend it only as an observation, that is all it is. In addition, the *Multi-Level System* is diametrically opposite to hypnosis, since we are intent on *increasing* the awareness of the subject, instead of trying to suppress it.

I remember one occasion, when I was conducting the regression of a woman who was having difficulty in getting impressions. I was giving her ideas of different possibilities of the location where the past life took place, and she finally agreed that it probably took place on or near water. I asked her to choose which it would be, and she said that it was probably on the water on a ship. I asked her what happened, and she told me she was in the water, drowning. I said, "Was there a fight on board the ship?" She corrected me and said, "No, a storm came up and it threw me overboard." From then on she was able to come up with good impressions, as she had locked in on the events properly, and felt the release when we finished the session.

The point of the foregoing is to demonstrate that your subject is *not* following suggestions furnished by you, but has within himself (or herself) the *true knowledge* of what happened, and is ready and able to correct you when you are wrong.

An important feature of this System is that the subject can take himself back, instead of relying on another person to conduct him. I believe it does help to have another person direct and ask questions, at least the first time a person is regressed. It allows the subject to concentrate within more easily, and having the healing energy flow from the conductor is certainly an added benefit.

The lack of a conductor's energy flow when you are by yourself can be corrected, since we are all *always* together through God. All you have to do, to get extra energy to help you when you are physically alone, is to mentally ask your spirit guides to give you the extra help, or one of the saints, or someone you know who is a healing channel. Then feel the energy come in, and proceed. To avoid draining a living person's energy, mentally ask permission of the person, and also visualize him taking in the extra energy needed and channeling it to you. Ask to be properly guided for best results.

Since this book is permanently charged with energy, you can also hold the book as you work alone. Don't worry about draining it of energy; it will replenish itself!

Much of the controversy about reincarnation is the question whether it is a Christian principle or not. Of course it is! The Christ power is Love! People have tuned in and used the life force, or creative power, throughout all of our past, to the beginning of the soul's creation! The reality of past lives, as shown here, is proof to me that love is eternal. You can feel the love, now, of those people you knew in your past lives, and it is still here in the present. Furthermore, as I said before, Padre Pio has been working with me and my clients, and helping me with my regression work. He has been seen standing behind me, as I work with those who come to me to realize more of their eternal existence. The "vibrations" of love and oneness often become very strong during these sessions, and at this moment of writing I feel Jesus' love within!

If you are a member of a healing group, it can be a definite benefit to a regression session. Have the members tune in to the healing energy, and channel it to both the conductor and the subject, with the intention to facilitate the process. Some of the members may also receive impressions of pertinent questions that should be asked about the subject's past life. The subject may also tune in to the group's power at any time when he is regressing himself.

　　　If you should be doing regressions on others, it would be a good idea to do some meditation on the project, and pray that you draw to you only those who can be helped by you.

CONCLUSION

　　Don't be too surprised if one of your "ordinary people" subjects regresses to a past life where he was a famous person. It happens occasionally. I believe it likely that most people have been, at some time, in one or more past lives, in a position of power, or famous in some manner. If "Ask and you shall be given" is a law, it is quite certain that many in the past have wished, "I wish I had the power that person has!," and thereby, in a subsequent lifetime, have been given that desired power. That soul will also learn, however, that it may be foolish to wish for something, when you do not know about the negative side of being in power, with all the responsibilities. In a like manner, others have wished (or asked) for fame; to be admired; any one of many similar possibilities. Thus, they are given a chance to experience those desires eventually. Then they also know the undesirable aspect of that type of life. I think that many such persons at the end of that lifetime would think, "Never again!," and thus return the next time to a more ordinary existence.

　　　Did you ever consider the possibility that the

solitary life of a hermit might be explained by a previous life, where he was very involved with many people, and needed a much-deserved rest? I think that you will find (as others have found) that there exists a tendency to swing from one extreme to the other, like a pendulum. It seems to me that the ideal situation for spiritual growth is to try to maintain more of a moderate existence, to attain better control of the lifetime. For the proper balance, each of us will probably experience living as both sexes, but not necessarily at the same time!

I believe that I have regressed at least one homosexual, and that the pattern has been carried over from a past life in the case I have in mind. Try to avoid condemnation of any person's lifestyle, since that action could lead to your experiencing the same problem in a future life. We all take different paths to attain our ultimate oneness with God!

This discourse is not really a "conclusion", since many of you (and hopefully myself, as well) will discover in this work other facets of our eternal life, that could be appended to this work. May God bless all who read and use this book!

-FINIS -

And a start for the new YOU.

ABOUT THE AUTHOR

Undoubtedly, many of my readers are going to wonder how this book came to be written, and what led me into this type of work. This is for the edification of such readers.

From a rather early age, I have been quite scientifically oriented in my thinking. I received my best grades in scientific subjects in high school. I still have my copy of *The Pocket Guide to Science,* which I received with a subscription to *Popular Science Monthly* in November of 1931. I was a freshman in Blanchardville High School in Wisconsin at the time, and I was already a science fiction fan, reading an occasional copy of *Gernsback's Wonder Stories* whenever I could get one at the drug store. This was not very often, as we did not have much money.

In 1934, while a junior in high school, I was introduced into the world of hypnotism. I borrowed an old pamphlet on the subject after seeing a demonstration at a tent show, which came to town every summer. I succeeded in hypnotizing a few of the kids I knew, then I set it aside for several years until I was overseas in China, near the end of World War II.

As a science fiction fan, I was wild about the wondrous workings of the minds of the Lensmen as conceived by "Doc" E. E. Smith.

I wrote for, and received introductory literature

I wrote for, and received introductory literature from, the Rosicrucians (AMORC), the Institute of Mentalphysics, and Frank B. Robinson's *Psychiana*. As I write this, I had not thought about the *Psychiana treatise* for many years. I did not pursue any of these teachings at that time, primarily for lack of funds.

When I was in India in 1944, I bought a book on Yoga in Bombay. It was Ramacharaka's *Fourteen Lessons on Yogi Philosophy*. Later, while in Shanghai, China, I had the privilege of meeting the now famous Indira Devi, Yoga teacher, who was at that time teaching in that city. One of her students was demonstrating Yoga postures, for her talk at the Foreign YMCA, on Bubbling Well Road. This was just across the street from the Race Course, where I was billeted in a Special Service dance band in the U.S. Army. She told me that she had all of the Ramacharaka books; I asked if I could borrow some to read. She was very gracious, and loaned a couple of them to me, and even gave one to me.

While I was in China, I joined the Rosicrucian Order (AMORC) in San Jose, after talking to one of the members of our radio installation team who was a member. After I was discharged from the Armed Forces in 1946, I came to Chicago to live, where I was a member and officer of the Nefertiti Lodge until I became inactive in the Rosicrucians in 1951.

My wife, Phyllis, and I were married on August 10 of 1946. (We have two sons; David is a musician and Don is a waiter). It was in June of the same year that I started to work for Zenith Radio Corp. I left Zenith in January of 1972.

When I was in Shanghai, I became interested in

prestidigitation, or magic. I received some instruction from two American soldiers, who were also magicians. I continued in magic when I got home, and joined the International Brotherhood of Magicians (a club composed of both amateurs and professionals), commonly known as IBM. Later, I joined the Mazda Mystic Ring, then located in Oak Park. I am a Past President and Life Member of this club, which now meets in Chicago.

I became proficient in a couple of areas of Magic... Giant Card Fans, and Paper Cutting. Both of these areas were somewhat ignored by the majority of magicians. Consequently, when I decided I would learn to form fans with Jumbo-size cards, I had to develop the handling techniques myself, as there were no other magicians in the Chicago area who were doing it. Today, I am still noted for the routine I developed, and still present. Many magicians, and other friends, know me as "Gerry Loe, Card Fan-atic." They know me partly for my specialty in doing card fans.

One day I conceived the idea of cutting a ring of five stars out of a piece of paper with one cut, and this led to my specialty in Paper Cutting. My book *Paper Capers* was published in 1955 by Magic, Inc., 5082 North Lincoln Ave., Chicago IL 60625. I learned to perform for any sized audience with ease, either for laymen or other magicians.

When I was given the opportunity to take the course in Advanced Perception several years ago I did so, but there were no major changes that I could see in myself at the time. In my particular case, my increase in psychic perception occurred more when I started to read Tarot cards.

Once one has taken the course in Advanced Perception (Institute-Center, P.O. Box 2856, Naperville, IL 60567-2856) one is free to attend subsequent classes as a refresher without charge, so I began attending again. The course is very comprehensive. Through seeming chance, I have met a number of people in unusual ways, which has served to get them into the classes. I began to do more healing, especially following the class sessions, and my healing abilities increased. It became easier and easier for me to direct and control the healing energy. My accuracy and helpfulness with the Tarot cards increased, and I taught several others to read, as well. I began to do readings at psychic fairs (or psyche-ins, as they are called in the Chicago area), and to do as much counseling as readings. For me, they go well together, along with healing.

I began to see that my training and experience as a magician and entertainer, and in being able to work easily in front of groups of people, would be valuable in lecturing and doing psychic work as well. In exchange, my control of energy as a healer has made me more dynamic as an entertainer.

From the response I have had to my few appearances on radio and television, there must be a very great number of people who are in need of help of all kinds. I realized that the problem-solving methods I use in my counseling should be made available to others, since they do work. We need more counselors, who care about their clients, to help in spreading the knowledge and applications of these and other workable techniques, to lift all who are ready to a higher level, if we can. Imagine what changes could occur in this world if most people fully realized that they are now creating their own futures by what they are doing and thinking; and that, when one is treating another in a particular manner, one is really doing it to one's self!

During the time I have been gathering material for this book, I have been on the lookout for other techniques that the ordinary person can use with a minimum amount of instruction, to help rectify many of the common problems that come up in life. I know that the techniques presented in this book are very effective when properly applied. One of the keys to effectiveness is to be persistent and consistent, without being "pushy" or too forceful. It is a law of the Universe that all forces must balance, so be careful of the forces you put out.

Some of the material given here suggests the possibility that some readers may make suitable counselors, if they are so inclined. It should be obvious that we are not all suited for giving good advice. If you have your own life well in order and have been able to solve your own problems, especially emotional ones, you may be the type of person whom we need in this world to help give some guidance to those less fortunate. The most important element in healing of any kind: physical, mental, emotional, etc., is your intention to heal. Therefore, if you have a strong desire to be a channel for God's blessings, you may become an effective healing channel, if you apply and dedicate yourself in that direction.

If you are contemplating doing counseling, you should get yourself a set of "repair tools," a group of techniques that you and your client can use to correct the cause of his or her problems, or to enable him or her to be of help to someone else. A few of my tools are given here. All of these are workable, but there is never any guarantee that they will always solve the problem to which they are applied. Each case is a separate entity, with its own variations and special aspects. When properly applied to a suitable problem, they do work. Use them consistently and persistently. It is imperative that all attitudes of condemnation and blame be set aside while using any of these methods.

Since the spectrum of abilities, devotion, and amount of energy supplied by various people varies over such a wide range, one cannot make a blanket statement that applying technique "A" for a specific number of days or weeks will solve the problem. This is where the use of divination as a guide can be of value in determining the time factor, and in correcting errors that creep in during application. Check readings can be made at any time to determine the state of progress of any situation.

It is usually a good idea to try out a technique yourself, before recommending it to others. Chances are that you will have things occur in your own life from time to time where you will have to use one of them to correct it, thus proving to you that it works. This has happened to me a number of times. Once you have made it work for you, you will feel more confident that the client can make it work for him. If you do not know immediately what the client should do to resolve his problem, by all means meditate on it before giving advice.

When you dedicate yourself to guidance of others, make a prayer and a decision that only those who can be helped by you will come to you for assistance. If you really mean it, this programming will work quite well. Those who cannot be helped by you will tend to be drawn to someone else, who can help them.

If you study and work with your dreams, some clues to problem-solving may come to you from them. Or you may possibly know instinctively what course to take. This often happens with me, when someone calls me, or comes to see me for assistance. It usually comes to me immediately, when my attunement is good. At other times I must meditate on it, or it may come to me when I am doing something else, and my mind is relaxed.

Two books which are useful in developing dream interpretation are *Dreams -- Your Magic Mirror*, by Elsie Sechrist, and *Edgar Cayce on Dreams*, published by Harmon Bros. Both are available at good book stores, or from the Association for Research and Enlightenment in Virginia Beach, VA 23451.

I cannot overemphasize the importance of becoming aware of the healing energy, or creative force, on a daily basis, or as a constant Presence. It can possibly transform your whole world for you!

You will
also enjoy

AS
YOU
THINKETH

The James Allen Classic brought into the 90's with a total revision and rewriting by award-winning, world-class motivational trainer, Dr. Tag Powell. Many call *As You Thinketh* the *"Handbook for Higher Living,"* for it holds the true answers for enjoyment of life and successful living, others call it *The Book of Vibrant Health,"* for it explains the true causes of good health, and how to obtain it, *"The Book of Instant Enlightenment,"* for it explains the real laws of the Universe, and the secrets of how to make these laws work for you. You might even call this work *"The Book of Answers,"* for it covers everything from how to take off weight to reaching the top of the achievement ladder; how to overcome circumstances to increasing your vision and ideals. Apply the techniques from this book and *it will* change your life for the better.

ISBN 0-914295-69-1
104 pages, Quality paperback $6.95

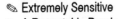